QIGONG

Qigong

essence of the healing dance

氣功

Garri Garripoli
and friends

Health Communications, Inc.
Deerfield Beach, Florida

www.hci-online.com

We would like to acknowledge the following publishers and individuals for permission to reprint the following material.

Material contributed by Duan Zhi Liang reprinted by permission of Duan Zhi Liang. ©1999 Duan Zhi Liang.
Material contributed by Wan Su Jian reprinted by permission of Wan Su Jian. ©1999 Wan Su Jian.
Material contributed by Luo You Ming reprinted by permission of Luo You Ming. ©1999 Luo You Ming.
Material contributed by Shi De Ren reprinted by permission of Shi De Ren. ©1999 Shi De Ren.
Material contributed by Kennerth S. Cohen reprinted by permission of Kenneth S. Cohen. ©1999 Kenneth S. Cohen.
Material contributed by Effie Poy Yew Chow reprinted by permission of Effie Poy Yew Chow. ©1999 Effie Poy Yew Chow.

(continued on page 319)

Library of Congress Cataloging-in-Publication Data
Garripoli, Garri, date.
    Qigong: essence of the healing dance—[Chi kung] / Garri Garripoli and friends.
        p.   cm.
    Parallel title in Chinese characters.
    Includes index.
    ISBN 1-55874-674-9
    1. chi Kung.   2. Exercise therapy.   I. Title. II. Title: Chi kung.
    RM727.C54G37   1999   99-22682
    613.7'1—dc21   CIP

©1999 by Garri Garripoli

ISBN 1-55874-674-9

Publisher: Health Communications, Inc.
            3201 S.W. 15th Street
            Deerfield Beach, FL 33442

Illustrations: Patrick Lugo
Calligraphy: Zhou Ai Qin
Design and Photography: Garri Garripoli

I dedicate this book to
Master Duan Zhi Liang, Master Luo You Ming,
Master Wan Su Jian, Master Effie Poy Yew Chow,
Master Guo Zhi Chen, Master Sha Zhi Gang,
Master Fan Fu Xiang, Master Zhang Yuan Ming,
Master Zhao Zheng Rong, Master Shi De Ren,
and all the other wonderful Qigong Masters
in China and around the world for having the faith
and open hearts to share their sacred knowledge
with me and all those who seek to make this
world a healthier and more loving place to live.
I also dedicate this book to my parents, Shirley
and Frank Garripoli, my first master teachers,
who guided my soul on its path.

Contents

Preface

This book is an expression of my heart. Qigong students and friends have been asking me to put my ideas down on paper for years. I am not a "form" oriented person, so the concept of slowing down ideas to print is a bit alien for me. What comes out during the classes I teach simply flows through me. I don't have the intellectual capacity or attitude that enables me to structure feelings and elusive concepts. It makes me think of a butterfly. Did you know that this creature would no longer be able to fly if you touched its wing and brushed off the delicate powder that is dusted upon it? The concepts related to Qigong and healing that I have written about in this book are a little like a butterfly's wings in that way—if you "touch" them too much, get too caught up in specific details, they may lose their ability to fly.

Lao-tzu, the ancient Taoist sage, wrote that "the Tao, the Natural Way, that could be described was no longer the Tao." This is a cryptic way of saying that things we feel on a deeply intuitive and emotional level about the working of the Universe can rarely be shared with mere words. By describing and "touching" on these ideas we have taken them from their pure state and are only left with mere replicas at best.

It is my hope that this book conveys the essence of the beautiful exercise and healing system of Qigong (pronounced "chee gung"). Even saying how it should be pronounced seems a bit foolish to me, like trying to put the net on that butterfly! But, as the philosopher Wittgenstein once wrote, "We live in a word-built world" and it is on this common ground that we must interact. The essence of Qigong can only be experienced through its practice. This book can then only serve to be an inspiration to help guide you to try this healing modality for yourself.

For the last two years I have been living in China, traveling throughout this magical country in search of the roots of Qigong. I have been studying Qigong and the Eastern energy healing arts since I was a teenager and it became clear to me to "drop everything" and go on this journey. Leaving stability and safety behind for the unknown sometimes seems like the only alternative in matters of the soul. The wonderful teachers that I met on my adventures shared openly with me and I am honored that they trusted my intention. Each of them made it very clear to me that when I returned to the West, I must teach. This book is an attempt at honoring that charge.

First, I try to give a little of the philosophical background that emerges from Qigong's ancient Chinese heritage. Next, I share some of the ancient and esoteric concepts related to this healing modality. Discussing children and Masters is an attempt at sharing my feeling that the fundamentals of Qigong are both naturally inherent in us, and at once complex and rich enough to take a lifetime to fully understand. As most of us are concerned with the practical application of any system's healing components, I share these thoughts which I have learned from a variety of Masters over the years.

I hope that through some of my personal experiences, and those of a variety of practitioners, you will understand how Qigong can motivate healing and inner transformation. Qigong cannot really be explained, it can only be experienced. The beauty of being human is that our uniqueness will carve for us personal conclusions as to what Qigong is. Outward descriptions of breathing techniques and specific movements only state the apparent. What happens within us during the Qigong experience is ours alone and creates for us a personal lexicon. This new language becomes the foundation for our personal growth and pathway to healing.

May the Qigong exercises that are presented in this book help you to see the variety of outward expressions that this system takes. They are typical of the thousands of forms which have developed over the millennia. It is only through trying moves like these with an open mind and heart that you will know whether Qigong is right for you. I realize that it can be difficult to learn moves just from reading. Special thanks to my friend Patrick Lugo for his illustrations in this section. They are meant more as "visual triggers" then instructional aids. I ask you to remain open and try. Our video can help you further and I hope that ultimately you will find a teacher if that is your path.

The script for my Public Television documentary on Qigong is included in this book since many of you have requested it. Written in a more straightforward manner than my sometimes poetic meanderings, it will present what is actually taking place in China today in the field of Qigong.

I have included a glossary and a resource section in the back of this book that I hope will assist you in further study.

Thank you for taking this journey with me, and for dancing between the words to always hear their truth and listen to their essence.

Peace.

Note: *When the names of organs are capitalized throughout this book, they refer to the acupuncture meridian energy system associated with that organ and not the organ specifically. Please remember that most of these words refer to theoretical and symbolic ideas that should not be misconstrued as actual physical locations. Though they refer to spots in the body, they are better thought of as "energy centers."*

One

Introduction

*I was sitting by the ocean one late sum-
mer afternoon, watching the waves
rolling in and feeling the rhythm of my
breathing, when suddenly I became
aware of my whole environment as being
engaged in a gigantic cosmic dance . . .
I "saw" cascades of energy coming down
from outer space, in which particles were
created and destroyed in rhythmic pulses;
I "saw" the atoms of the elements and
those of my body participating in this
cosmic dance of energy; I felt its rhythm
and I "heard" its sound, and at that
moment I knew that this was the Dance
of Shiva, the Lord of Dancers, worshiped
by the Hindus.*

Fritjof Capra

3

A single, dancing thread ties the people of the world together into a cohesive fabric. This is our humanness and mortality. We are all born with a similar challenge, borne from the blessing of ownership of this complex physical body. No one escapes this common karma. That's part of the trip of life on this planet. With this ownership, or should I call it "rental," comes the sometimes immense responsibility of health maintenance. For some, this task goes by almost unnoticed, save the required food and water going in and waste products coming out. This is a charmed karma, of course. For the rest of us, stewardship of this incredible biological machinery takes constant attention. It doesn't matter whether our skin is dark brownish or yellowish or reddish or whitish or any combination. It doesn't matter if our genetic makeup affords us a small, slender carriage or a large, dense one. The fact remains, inside we vary very little. This is one thing that ties us, that binds our souls to one another. We all can relate to headaches, to bellyaches, to sprains, to being tired. We all can relate to the challenge and fears of disease. Our ultimate death secures our mortality and, thus, gives value and sacredness to life.

The ride that is this life reminds us that the body is but a leg of the tripod that upholds our existence. Married to a soul and a mind, the body provides us with carnal pleasures and serves to reflect our overall spiritual and mental condition like a polished mirror. Secured to a mind and a body, the soul can begin to express itself fully through the myriad experiences it needs on this Earth. Married to a body and a soul, the mind can soar as it gathers knowledge and carves our path of self-discovery. Within this three-legged creature, we dance. To the extent that we can discover our own, unique balance, we are whole . . . and once whole, we can truly dance like the free spirits we are. Qigong (Chi Kung) calls us to the dance floor of life.

Qigong (pronounced "chee gung") is an ancient Chinese health-care system. The word Qigong is made up of the Chinese character *Qi*, which can mean *breath* or *energy*, and *Gong*, which can mean *exercise* or *work*. Qigong can be thought of as "breath exercise" or "energy work." Its roots can be traced back thousands of years, from inscriptions on tortoise shells, carbon-dated back to 2,500 B.C., and to silk drawings of exercise movements found in tombs some four thousand years old. These windows on the past reveal that human nature hasn't changed all that much—our need to slow down and get in touch with our body, mind, and spirit was as evident then as it is now. To slow down, to become at peace with ourselves is the key to healing. Similar to Yoga, and actually the foundation of Tai Chi, Qigong is a combination of exercise and meditation. It can be thought of as a "moving meditation." Qigong uses deep, diaphragmatic breathing in conjunction with slow, synchronous, Tai Chi-like movements to bring our body, mind, and spirit into alignment and balance. It is estimated that over 80 million people practice Qigong regularly in China today.

Qigong can be done either standing, lying down, or sitting. I have worked with many invalids who were bound
to a bed or wheelchair and found they could
perform simple Qigong movements and breathing exercises to help bring their energy into balance. When this
balance is achieved, stress is reduced. Relieving this stress
on our being increases our immune system, helping us
ward off illness. It reduces blood pressure, helps our
organs operate more efficiently, and can bring great
improvements to our overall mood. Research indicates
that regular Qigong practice and treatment can eliminate
chronic pain and symptoms, reduce the need for medication, shorten postoperative recovery time, effectively
control diabetes, and even reduce the size of or eliminate
tumors. Tests in China show that students who practice
Qigong actually score higher than control groups that
don't practice.

Stress is something that we are not always conscious
of; it can exist on a cellular level and hide, masked by
our ingrained insensitivity. The results of stress usually
become evident when it's too late. Qigong is both a pre-
ventative modality and a treatment system. Learning this
system to better your own health will inevitably assist you
in treating others that are out of balance, physically and
spiritually. Medical Qigong is the practice of using your
own Qi (or Chi, pronounced "chee") field, through the
movement of your hands and conscious intention, to
guide the Qi of Nature into your patient and catalyze the
healing process. Qigong teaches the power of the

unseen. It brings us in touch with Qi, the energy of life. Qigong reminds us of the intense power of thought and intention. Evidence continues to support that patients with a positive attitude heal quicker than patients in a stressed condition. Negative energy in the workplace will always show as a drop in productivity. Qigong practice brings you into a relaxed state with its deep breathing that superoxygenates your body. Unlike strenuous, aerobic exercises that raise adrenaline but burn energy reserves, Qigong's slow movements build and store more Qi than the amount required to do the exercise. This helps to energize you overall and bring more oxygen to the brain. The quality and essence of our thinking affects not only ourselves, but it affects people and things around us. Practicing Qigong with regularity can bring you in touch with the common sense that is your nature, a common sense that is becoming less and less common as the pace and pressures of life continue to increase. How we feel and what we think has a powerful and direct effect on our world . . . and on our ability to heal. The ancient sages of China believed that *thinking* was a form of Qi, so the quality of our thoughts reflects the quality of our Qi. Thoughts and attitude have a very powerful influence on not only our own bodies, but everyone and everything around us. Qigong reminds us of this in a very tangible way as its slow movements and deep breathing helps to get us in touch with our connection to the world around us. Qigong is a strategy for freedom from our cage of isolation.

The pursuit of freedom burns within each of us, fundamental to our existence as humans. It is mapped on to every one of us like a spiritual genetic code. Within our sameness, our souls dictate a uniqueness. Fueled by our individual karma, freedom expresses itself specifically and uniquely for each of us. The mind, our manifest ego, serves to infuse the individual dose of fear each of us requires to follow our own path, our destiny of sorts. It is probably freedom from this essential fear that is our life lesson. That's just my theory, but I have yet to see otherwise. When we act out of fear, we are under the ego's control. The ego is fear. It is that force that leads us to the false notion that we are alone in the Universe, alone in the struggle of survival. The ego, working through the mind, turns a cold shoulder to messages from the body and turns a deaf ear on the soul. Qigong practice can help us to regain our sensitivity to these signals. It can bring us back to our connection with the Universe. It can remind us we are not alone. To be fully alive, we need to dance . . . and to dance, the partners must move together, as one.

To live in harmony as a civilization, as a nation, as a community or as a couple, we must first live in harmony as a self. This is our ultimate responsibility if we wish to live to our full potential. In every culture, sages are revered for their ability to live in harmony with Nature and with themselves. The outward reflects the inward. It was the great, ancient sages who discovered the acupuncture meridians, the principles of Qigong and the healing qualities of herbs. They knew this information through their intuitive connection with Nature. To live in harmony with Nature, we pursue a harmony of Mind, Body and Soul. To be in balance as a self, we are moved to be in harmony with Nature.

The ancient Taoists of China saw living according to the Tao, the Natural Way, as both sociological and eco-logical. To these spiritually minded people, the dance of life was all-encompassing; nothing escaped the Tao as the Tao moved all things. To honor this nameless and formless force you simply needed to live a virtuous life based on harmonious existence with the world around you. It didn't matter if you were in the country or the city, if you were a butcher or an emperor, the Way permeated all things everywhere. To discover the Way, the harmo-nious path, in whatever you do, is your charge. Taoist Qigong traditionally emphasizes the body; nature and the physical world are sacred. To honor this, Taoist monks never cut their hair, even to this day. The Taoist attitude strives for a strong body, focusing on longevity tech-niques. With a strong body, a balanced spirit emerges naturally.

The second pillar of Chinese thought is Buddhism. The ancient Buddhist sages lived by the scriptures of the Buddha, the Enlightened One. Gautama Buddha, an aver-age man, was their inspiration. Buddha achieved enlight-enment by transcending the limits set by society, by his family, by his human fears. No longer was he alone in his struggle as a human. He saw our common challenges and weaknesses, how each of us faced similar monsters. By letting go of desire, we become free. Though the details of how desire expresses itself may differ from person to person, the essence is the same. Some may need to let go of material security, while others need to release their attachment to control or fear. With this letting go comes freedom—and the start of our uniquely personal dance. Traditional Buddhist Qigong placed its emphasis on the spirit. Through meditation and inward calm, the Chinese Ch'an (derived from the Sanskrit *dhyana* and translated as "meditation") Buddhists believed that developing a pure spirit results in a healthy body.

The Chinese people have always accepted these two philosophies as complementary and, in fact, necessary to have a balanced view of the world. They move with ease between the two schools of thought, knowing that each helps explain an integral aspect of our lives.

Moving with ease within the physical constraints of our temple of muscle and bones is the subject of this book. The theory of moving freely is at the core of Qigong, since on the surface, it seems like a simple stretching and exercise system. Qigong has its roots not only in China's ancient philosophies of Taoism and Buddhism, but in Traditional Chinese Medicine (TCM) as well. When the blood, lymph, limbs and Qi all move smoothly, we are considered to be in good health. Qi is that intangible energy that animates the human body and all things in this Universe. Richard Lee, founder of the China Healthways Institute, refers to it as "bioelectric-vitality," while others call it "life force." Western languages don't even have a word to translate the Chinese "Qi" character. This points to a vast difference in the way people of these two cultures view the world. It is a beautiful character (the top one of the two on the cover of this book) composed of two radicals in its pre-simplified form. One is the character for uncooked rice. The other represents the concept of steam or vapor. This shows the Yin and Yang aspects of energy. Yin, form and Earth, are depicted in uncooked rice. Yang, formlessness and Heaven, are portrayed in steam. When both meet, the rice is cooked and can be used to generate energy; in other words, it can be eaten. Chinese characters are stories in and of themselves, concepts that transcend a simple one-word translation. Qi is a process that requires raw elements which come together in a dynamic reaction. As humans, we require food and drink to generate Qi. Their quality are reflected in the quality of the Qi we generate. Every interaction we have with people and things also contributes to the quality of our Qi. The kind of people and things you associate with are reflected in the quality of your Qi. The way all things interface, animate and inanimate, dictates the texture of Qi in the world around us. Qi is a dance in itself. It is the energy that animates the Universe.

In the West, the body/mind debate has gone unresolved since the days of ancient Greece. It has created a dualism of physicality and nonphysicality. In China, body/mind and even spirit are seen as aspects of a whole that is indivisible. Each part, like a hologram, reflects the whole.

This is what I call the Body Mirror theory, which pos-
tulates that our body reflects all of who we are. It is a
window into our state of mind, the condition of our soul
and our general health. As we come to accept that we are
truly a composite of mind, body and soul, the health and
well-being of all three aspects of our being must always
be taken into account. To look at one without the others
is to deny our humanness. As a society, we are coming
to accept that the mind has a powerful effect on the
body. Once we understand that the state of our body
affects the state of our mind and soul, many things in our
life come into focus. We become much more conscious
of our diet, as what we eat and drink clearly affects our
mental and emotional states. We become much more
conscious that stiffness and aches in the body mirror
inflexibility and imbalance in the mind and spirit. We all
accept that body language is a powerful communicating
aspect of who we are. I consider this a large aspect of the
Body Mirror and one of the most powerful tools we have
at our disposal for self-awareness. To study the Body
Mirror requires commitment and honesty. The commitment is to breaking patterns that we have adopted in our
daily lives. Qigong places great importance on our
breathing. Practicing its deep, slow breathing helps to
slow us down enough to gain balance in our mood and
attitude. It's like the way a friend will remind you to stop
and take a deep breath before attempting a challenge.
Our breath races when we are nervous and is shallow
when we are ill. It is a powerful indicator of our state of

mind. Learn to guide your breath and you will gain control of one of your life's patterns that now controls you. These patterns may manifest in the way we hold our body at rest, the way we lean forward when we walk, or the way we cover our mouth when we talk. Qigong puts great emphasis on relaxed posture and efficient, intentional body movement; both during practice and throughout our day. It requires a commitment to seeing beyond the limits of our ego and working toward a more objective view of ourselves. This leads to the need to be honest, to admit to ourselves when we see how a posture or action reflects an attitude, a fear or a repressed emotion.

This kind of self-observation was a focus in the Fourth Way School developed by G. I. Gurdjieff and his students such as P. D. Ouspensky and Thane Walker. Gurdjieff adopted many concepts from the Sufi mystics of Persia, a school that pursued enlightenment through self-awareness. This *self* was one connected intimately with the Creator, free in body and spirit. The Sufi Whirling Dervishes used dance, which, as the name suggests, spun the dancer into an ecstatic state of reverie—a complete sensual experience involving the body, mind and soul.

This, too, is the essence of Qigong. Practicing the gentle movements of Qigong while synchronizing them with deep, diaphragmatic breathing, you may discover you are able to enter into an ecstatic state. This is a natural and culturally universal experience. When we understand the essence of a thing or a system, its connection to all things becomes apparent. We are transported to a melding of awareness, to a deep relationship with the Tao, or the Natural Way, of life. Qigong then becomes more of a code word, a metaphor for a basic system of self-preservation. If you understand and practice Qigong's fundamental precepts of fluid movement and deep breathing, you will find correlations with other healing systems. Many students have brought this to my attention, and I'm always glad to see they've made that crucial connection to essence. It is important to honor different systems, to know them deeply and to take them into your soul. In this way, we are transformed. We have moved beyond intellectual knowledge and entered that space of emotional and spiritual soul connection.

Western science has begun to understand the value of thinking with both hemispheres of the brain. The left hemisphere is associated with linear thinking and abstractions such as mathematics, while the right hemisphere of the brain is mostly responsible for our creative and artistic abilities. The Yin and Yang of our mental capacity, these two hemispheres, is linked by a gray mass known as the corpus callosum. It seems to facilitate interaction between these two regions of the brain. When it is damaged, our ability to grasp whole concepts is impaired. In some ways, Qigong plays the same role as this gray matter. Through the simple and subtle elements of Qigong, the breath and the body move in concert. This slow synchrony has the catalytic effect of triggering our innate ability to grasp the totality and unity of the

Universe. Maybe for a moment we get a glimmer of that sense of Oneness. Maybe while we are in the Qigong State, we have a profound awareness of balance; maybe a shift in our energetic matrix takes place and our life completely changes. Qigong is very personal and, as such, each of us will experience something uniquely ours. The key to enter that state is allowing your natural flow to begin. The Tao, the Natural Way, will impress itself on you like a loving embrace if you give it a chance. The Buddha will enter you as a ship enters a safe harbor if you create the environment. We are malleable creatures, a double-edged sword that seeks our own mastery. Without this intent, we continue to be molded by society, by a system based on lonely fear. A system that judges and compares, a system that rewards conformity and mediocrity.

Qigong is a tool to help us transcend these limits. It provides a mechanism by which we can realign the workings of our life. It requires your total involvement, as any serious pursuit should consume you while you are involved in it. As Qigong is essentially beyond form, beyond time, how you actually bring yourself into Qi state is immaterial. Some may tell you to practice stillness for several hours while others may have you practice specific forms in sequence at certain times of the day. My teachers whom I resonate most deeply with all agree that it is the intent you hold while practicing that is most important. It doesn't matter for how long or what time of day you practice. Our ultimate clarity comes from transcending form and moving beyond the shackles of space and time. Clinging to these things is counter-productive to your spiritual growth. Practice and honor a system, whatever the form. Know it until you can sense whether it is right for you. Trust your bones; trust your muscles. The Body Mirror reflects both ways; your body will communicate with your mind as much as your mind guides your body. Conscious movement speaks to your soul. This is the secret of healing. Specific movements, hand positions (*mudras*), sounds (*mantras*), and visuali-zations can be healing triggers. They shift energy, har-monizing Qi. Yet it is important to remember that its effectiveness depends on the individual. We are a delicate web of emotion, karma and Qi—a myriad of forces that define our ever-changing energy field. Some people change over decades, others in a matter of hours; the amorphous cycles are individual, and this is part of our self-discovery. The Body Mirror tells us we but have to listen. When we understand our rhythms and our evolve-ment, we can change accordingly.

This is living with the Tao. The same dance on a dif-ferent scale. We are constantly being asked to let go of our clinging, to transcend linearity. What we hold onto for safety and security may be precisely what holds us back from growth. What we stand for can sometimes be what we hide behind; what we intently repeat may pro-hibit us from moving ahead. My dear Qigong and Kung Fu teacher Master Duan Zhi Liang of Beijing is fervent about mixing up the order of the eighteen Wuji Qigong forms. When I began under his tutelage, I had years of training in Tai Chi, an experience that played into my need for accomplishment. In a world that seemed a bit crazy and unmanageable, perfecting my Tai Chi forms and repeating the prearranged sequence provided a sense of pride and security. Master Duan entered my life with his chaos theory and turned everything on its head. This ninety-two-year-old Qigong Master never did anything in the same way or order twice. As we practiced the Wuji Qigong forms, he liked to sing do-re-me-fa-so-la-ti-do. Then he'd laugh and sing fa-do-so-re-me-do-la-ti. Formlessness . . . he made it very clear that it was important to mix things up, to add a calculated amount of chaos to a situation. This applied to the sequence that we practiced the eighteen forms as well. When you don't give your mind the chance to hold on to anything, it lets go of its hold. When the mind lets go, we begin our path to freedom. When the mind lets go, we become present and we can act naturally, instinctively, soulfully. This is the apparent magic of Qigong's healing power. Freedom to let go into natural balance. TCM theory states that all pain and disease arise from either stagnant or excessive Qi. This imbalance has its roots in our diet, lifestyle, genetics, emotional state, the weather or myriad other influences on our life. The dedicated practice of Qigong begins to bring our life into balance. With this balance comes good health—of the body, mind and spirit. I think of Qigong as sensitivity training. As we start "feeling" our Qi, we begin to have a greater sense of the influences that affect us. We begin to learn our limits. We begin to learn our limitlessness.

Though its roots are uniquely Chinese, Qigong is a health-care system that touches our very soul and thus transcends cultural barriers. I have practiced Qigong with people whose roots lie deep in Africa and others who have emerged from traditional Christian Russia. I have practiced with people steeped in Hindu heritage and those who honor their ancient Judaic roots. I have practiced with people who are planted in working-class America and with children who were free of any cultural definitions. Each explored Qigong and discovered its healing benefits and the common ground that ties us all together. This is my prayer for Qigong practice: that people can truly understand the essence of Qi and see how we are one people, unique yet fundamentally alike, bound by a common and universal force.

Two

The Dance

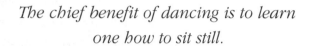

*The chief benefit of dancing is to learn
one how to sit still.*

Samuel Johnson

In my research throughout China, I found
that experts agree that the inner, meditative aspects of Qigong emerged from the
ancient mystical traditions of Taoism,
Buddhism and the animistic spiritualism
that preceded them. The outward expression of Qigong, they say, comes from
primitive Dao Yin dances. These were
amongst the various tribal rituals and cus-
toms of many villages. They survived
throughout the generations because they
had a very practical aspect. They helped
alleviate aches and pains, presumably from
rheumatoid arthritis that was common
among those who worked in the rice paddies and in other damp conditions. Dance
is part of nearly every culture, playing its

21

role in courtship and mating rituals, artistic expression and entertainment. Physicians recommend ballroom dance to the elderly to help keep their bodies limber. Young people flock to dance clubs as if driven by an unseen force. Dance is a way for us to freely express ourselves, to feel young again.

Qigong reminds us to be like a baby, soft and pliable. It was a time when our legs could bend back so our toes could go in our mouth. Our skull plates were not yet nearly fused together; our skin was supple. We had few toxins in our bodies. Our voice was strong. Our bellies were full and round, dense with Jing Qi, that energy core empowering us to grow. Anyone could see our soul through our eyes. This mirrored a spirit that was needy, yet free to live by the drive of those basic instincts and nothing artificial. There were no masks apart from the body itself; self-awareness didn't yet exist. Everyone admired your beauty; they were reminded of the gift of life each time you held on to their finger with a strong grip, each time you stared at something with your complete focus, each time you cried to exercise your lungs and express hunger. Qigong returns us to this simplicity, to our essential nature. It brings us to that soul we long to embrace, seen darkly through the fog of the ego as it struggles for dominance, like a child fighting for a few more minutes of television-watching before getting some needed evening sleep.

Maybe it was that child in me that needed to be nurtured when I walked away from my successful business a few years ago and decided to live in China. It was time for a cleansing of sorts. I had come to a place in my life where I needed to secure my dedication to my beliefs. I had to face a lot of fears in the process, but on a soul level, I realized I had no choice. I only knew a few words of Mandarin, but I traveled across China propelled by my hope of meeting sincere Qigong teachers. Synergetic forces conspired to bring me in touch with Masters in the most curious of ways. I am honored to have been accepted by so many beautiful people. One day, while riding on a bus in Beijing, I heard an old man with a long white beard humming a tune. It was a melody I hadn't heard since going to church as a child. I began humming with him. He turned and smiled. When he got up to leave the bus, he gestured for me to leave with him. Why not, I thought . . . we went to a park and I soon realized I was with Master Duan, my new Qigong and Kung Fu teacher.

Master Duan is many things to many people, fulfilling the notorious role of an elder teacher. The master's game is one of movement—sometimes internal and sometimes external. Master Duan moves in the grand dance, flowing from situation to situation with a confident elegance painted in humble strokes. One evening, after a particularly long day of workouts, I found myself in a joyous celebratory gathering outside of Beijing. It was composed of several Masters and a large entourage of students from China and Japan. With the energy up, somebody asked me to teach everyone the *macarena*, a Latin-inspired dance routine that was making big rounds in America.

Amidst Qigong and Kung Fu Masters—and students as proficient in a variety of moving forms as any Master—I shared this simple dance, thinking to myself that it was too pedestrian, too trite for this dedicated crowd. Watching the serious intent of everyone bent on trying to learn this basic routine opened my heart to the level of focus in this crowd. They didn't judge this dance as just another commercial craze as I did. For them, it was a form to be absorbed and honored, as if it was part of my revered tradition. They were "in the moment," and this dance consumed them as they became it. People who were proficient in complex Shaolin Kung Fu combinations stumbled over the macarena's progression until they made it part of their very being. Like a flock of birds moving as one, the group finally locked in and became macarena experts. With this level of comfort at hand, they became jovial and they returned to being their childlike selves, laughing and carrying on. Watching the process of transformation was amazing.

Master Duan then gestured for everyone to open up a circular area amidst the crowd and pulled me in with him. We both did the macarena to the backbeat that had now repeated what seemed like a hundred times on the stereo. He then slowly modified the dance with hysterically funny gestures, ranging from holding his nose to grabbing his butt. Then he engaged me in a hybrid macarena/push hands routine. Liquid change from entertainment to a martial arts exercise. That elegant expression of moving from one state to another without missing a beat. He turned a simple dance into a lesson; you could hear the crowd acknowledging this as they watched. The Dance. Always changing, infused with the intent of the dancers. . . .

Master Duan dances Qigong. He moves as if entranced in a tango with the Universe. In a one on one with students, he draws you into his undulation. In this way, you learn how he directs his Qi flow throughout his body. Every move he makes is a lesson. This is the charge of a true Master. After a long day training a group of students in Wuji swordplay, he asked me to organize an evening dance. In a secluded hotel nestled on a lake far from any city, I transformed a meeting room into a dance hall as best I could. The students came, expecting a frivolous party and began to mill around. Duan appeared, in his typical, long and flowing traditional garb, and began to take people onto the dance floor one at a time. Watching the faces of each person as they completed their experience was precious. A glazed stare and a nod of understanding attached to each person. Several women came up to me and secretly told me they had never danced with such a sensual partner as the ninety-two-year-old Master Duan.

This is the essence of Qigong: a total absorption of the senses and spirit. With this absorption comes a rebalancing. What was most out of balance in our life seems to make itself known to our awareness. A Master is akin to a profound experience embodied. A true Master commonly can trigger the awakening and realization of our realignment. That Master Duan moves like a dancer simply reflects his attitude toward life. He uses the Chinese word *hundun* when he refers to his family's system of Qigong. This word closely resembles the English word "chaos." Through chaos, we learn stillness. Through chaos we learn that everything is in a state of flux. By embracing chaos, we embrace the Tao. Immerse yourself in the chaos, flow with the natural energies around you and experience the freedom of your being.

It becomes evident in Qigong practice that our body is a field generator. As we move our body in Qigong exercise, we become conscious of how waving our arms and hands in a specific way can have an effect on the rest of our body. We also become conscious of how this can have an effect on someone else. Our body generates fields of many radiation types, from heat to light. It generates Qi. It generates probability, more commonly thought of as karma. These emissions happen naturally but it is believed that through practices such as Qigong, we can enhance and focus this radiation. Key points in our body emit, receive, store and generate Qi more than others. All points in our body can do these things actually, it's just that some are more easy to observe at the novice level. The glossary in this book will discuss some of these points.

When we practice Qigong, we use our breath to build Qi and to regain a sense of balance and focus. Breathe deep. Pause for a moment and simply breathe deep. While you read these words, you can be practicing

Qigong. Breathe deep. Get in touch with your breath. This is the technique fundamental to healing and meditative systems in nearly every culture. Breathe deep. It brings us in touch with our body and soul in such a complete way. Breathe deep.

I won't go into the dozens of ways that I've learned to breathe as I don't feel it ultimately matters. Breathe deep. Suck in your belly and diaphragm as far as you can while you exhale. Extend your belly and diaphragm when you inhale. Breathe deep. Qigong can literally translate from the Chinese as "breath work" in one sense. Breathe deep. Imagine energy, Qi, coursing through your body with each exhale. Imagine Qi filling your body through every pore as you inhale. Breathe deep. Master Duan reminds me that it is good to keep your mouth gently closed and only breathe through your nostrils, but he is also quick to remind me that we must become conscious of breathing through our skin while we play Qigong. I remember from my premed courses that the skin is in fact the largest respiratory organ. Breathe deep. Let your shoulders drop, allow a wave of calm to pass through your body. Breathe deep. Expand the image of your body to extend deep into the planet and far into space. Breathe deep. Sense the connection of your being to all things; we are a unified field of infinite energy. Breathe deep. Allow your heart to smile. Breathe deep. This is Qigong.

When we have achieved this state, we can begin moving through various forms. As our arms glide around us, our hands pass through our field of Wei Qi, or "external"

Qi. Imagine the effect of a magnet passing near iron
filings, or the way hair reacts to static electricity. I sometimes see it as if my hands were moving through smoke,
watching the turbulence of the smoke swirl and part as I
pass through it. At a point, you may feel as if you are
moving through a viscous fluid, thick and syrupy. There
is "something" in the "nothing." This is Wuji: that point
where "something" and "nothing" collide.

Qigong requires creative visualization, which is why
children respond so well to it. I've also found that the
elderly seem to flow easily with guided visualization. My
experiences teaching Qigong in convalescent homes
bring tears to my eyes. People who are regarded as hopeless are left in wheelchairs, lined up against walls as if
they are potted plants. Fed and generally cared for, they
are missing the vital component that they crave. The
touch, movement and mental stimulation of Qigong
enlivens even the tough cases. I recall a staff member
telling me to bypass a particular woman resident because
she couldn't raise her arms and was not "in touch with
reality." I've never been good at being told something
isn't possible, so I worked with her anyway. I began a
guided visualization with her, creating an image of her
body that extended far beyond her skin, far beyond the
room. She never broke her gaze into my eyes as I spoke
to her. Soon her arms were way above her head, and she
started laughing out loud. "I really can't do this you
know," she said. Her breath was short from her years of
being so sedentary, but her effort was so present. She

kept laughing and said she hadn't felt so free in years. The whole staff stood and gaped. Sometimes, all people need is a guide to lead them toward their own ability to travel. I remember how vital my imagination needed to be during the convalescence of my own crippled legs. Students will sometimes query whether it's all just "in their mind." I ask them to tell me what isn't . . .

The first step in sensing Qi is to imagine it. Before we go on vacation, don't we *first* imagine how beautiful that Mediterranean beach is going to be? Once it dances around our mind for a while, the details get worked out and eventually we're walking in the sand listening to some romantic Italian songs lilt in the background. Everything starts with imagination, and Qigong is no different.

Making the transition from imagination to practical application is where your dedication and sincerity comes in. Even after all these years, sometimes I have my doubts; it's a funny human trait. I've spent my life con cerned with these issues of applying metaphysical con- cepts to real-world use. If you can't take what you learned on the mountain and apply it at the bus stop, as the Fourth Way mystic Gurdjieff once said, then what worth does it have?

I was at the hospital last evening, another long night there for my family as a relative was being treated for painful symptoms caused by an ailment the Western doc- tors couldn't pinpoint. She couldn't sleep and things hadn't changed for twenty-four hours. No physicians

were available until morning, and it looked grim. I began
to work on her with Qigong for about twenty minutes.
The nurse on duty came in, took a look at me, smiled and
left. I remember having that brief feeling that digs at me,
wondering if this really is going to help in a case as bad
as this. It was time for guests to leave and I went out into
the cold night air, maintaining my imagery of balance and
peace. My wife Daisy stayed on, as she had to translate
the Chinese Toisanese dialect to English in case of emergency. She told me the next morning that our relative
slept through the night, without symptom or pain.
Another reminder to trust and don't let your questioning
intellect interrupt something far beyond its grasp.

When we practice Qigong, whether on another person
or on ourselves, we invoke natural energy shifts that are
well within the realm of accepted physics. There seems
to be a multitude of events occurring simultaneously. A
reaction takes place between the fields of Qi generated
between body parts and between bodies. Certain key
points, such as the Lao Gong point in the palm of the
hand, seem to generate more Qi than others. When the
palm is passed over an area of the body—it doesn't matter if it's yours or another's—the change in density of the
Qi field creates effects on a cellular level. This area of
research has only scratched the surface of our understanding about what actually happens. Every action has
its effects in this world. We accept that "every action has
an equal and opposite reaction." This is proven in physics
equations. Just because we can't measure the subtlety

of the "equal and opposite reaction" with Qigong we shouldn't dismiss it. Our challenge should be to develop our intuitive sensitivity so that we can learn to sense Qi shifts when they occur. In the meanwhile, I believe we should allow our imagination and intuition to guide us as we practice and treat. Please, please consult a physician in any case that is severe or lingering.

When you practice a Qigong move for your own health maintenance, imagine that your hand is passing through a field of energy. Imagine what it would feel like. Get specific with your descriptions because the more "real" you make it, the more you will assist yourself in the process of enhancing your perception. This will help open your receptivity. It will give you the permission to "feel" what's occurring on the subtle levels. When you pass your palm over parts of your body, remind yourself that reactions are occurring. Begin to "see" them, to "feel" them. Be gentle with yourself if you don't sense anything at first. Just trust that you must activate your imaginative centers. This is about letting go . . . letting go of a lifetime's worth of illusion. Maybe you'll find that this new "illusion" becomes more real than what you have been used to. For this is where healing actually occurs.

Everyone senses Qi in different ways. Each person has his or her own way of perceiving things. Some may see Qi, some may feel Qi. What they see and feel are also very subjective. When you practice Qigong exercises like the ones in this book, you may come to discover your own abilities. Some people are never able to perceive Qi in a tangible way, they simply trust their results and a sense that they get about blockage and density. You can only learn these things through practice. A teacher can tell you to pass your hand over your body or that of a person in pain, and try to sense Qi flow. The rest is up to you and it takes time and experience to get to the point of being sensitive. Everyone's capacity to heal themselves or others is different. I have found, though, that everyone has this innate gift. With Qigong healing, gently passing the palm of your hand a few inches over the point of pain for a few minutes and then slowly moving your palm a few feet away from this point can prove to be incredibly valuable.

When you use these techniques to treat another person, treat them the same way as if you were working on yourself. The only factor that is a bit different is that the other person is generating a field that is imbalanced to a degree that is different than yours. You, then, must bring your being into a balanced state, as this helps catalyze your patient's balance. This can be done with a few minutes of Qigong breathing and movement. Like a harmonizing sound wave that creates a sympathetic vibration in nearby objects (guitar strings do this to other strings as well as the body of the guitar; opera singers can actually break glass if they hit the right note), your Qi affects those around you. This is important to remember whether you are consciously treating someone or not.

Another theory that I've learned from many Masters who are effective in their healing is the concept of Qi density distribution. It's a simple idea that works for a lot of people. It is thought that holding your palm *near* a part of your or someone else's body creates a high-density Qi field. It follows that holding your palm *away* from the body creates a low-density field. This is the basic idea. Hold or slowly pass one hand near a body part while holding your other hand away by extending your arm and facing your palm upward. Experiment. This is the only way to learn. It is healthy to study many different Qigong systems, and you should to gain experience. It's not that any one is better than any other, it's just that some will resonate for you and thus prove more effective in your work.

To discover the health benefits of balancing your system, you must be sincere in your pursuit of Qigong. This doesn't just mean doing your prescribed movements for an hour or two each day. It means bringing the principles of Qigong into the basic activities that consume your life. Imagine turning a drive in your car into a Qigong exercise. With each step that you would normally take in a semiconscious way, bring consciousness to it. Link a deep breath to it. Perform each step slowly and deliberately. Reach for the door handle . . . breathe out. Pull it toward you . . . breathe in. Sit down on the seat . . . breathe out. Hold your key . . . breathe in. Put the key in the ignition . . . breathe out. Turn the key . . . breathe in. Hold the steering wheel . . . breathe out. Link a breath with an action. This will slow . . . you . . . down. It will bring you to a deeper connection with things you take for granted. It will synchronize your breath with your intention. It will teach you to listen to the Tao. This is Qigong.

Take the time to give it a chance. Learn how out of sync we are in our lives, how out of step we are with our energy flow. Listen with your heart. If it is right for you, a space will open up . . . and you will enter.

Three

Qi Space

Movement overcomes cold,
stillness overcomes heat.

Tao Te Ching

I am amazed at how unique we are. During the Qigong classes I teach, I am constantly reminded of this. I ask students to hold their hands a few inches apart at waist level while standing in a relaxed position in order to begin the process of sensing Qi [see Wuji Qigong form called *Xun* on page 246]. We continue this until everyone in the class feels something. I never say *what* you should feel as it is a very subjective experience. I love it when students share what they felt. The responses are varied and individual. I've heard things such as "sponge-like" and "magnetic" . . . and everything in between. Some talk of feelings and sensations while others are reminded of something from childhood.

Philosophers enjoy discussing how each of us holds a unique image of reality, and thus the world is nothing but a myriad of unique realities. Each of our world views dictates our own take on this life. What we carry in our belief system works to create the world we experience. The common knowledge base that we have all agreed upon, consciously or unconsciously, provides a way for us to share this planet together. Everything outside of this is up for grabs.

When you think about it, what lies outside the agreed-upon is vast, as the Universe is truly infinite. It is here where the fun really begins. In this place, we have no common language, we have no lines of demarcation. Definition is amorphous. In this place, we find Qi. I like to call it "Qi Space."

How is it that for some people, life appears effortless, while for others it is a constant tragedy? How is it that several people can attempt a challenge with no success and someone comes along and does it almost without trying? How is it that some people die from a disease while others outlive their diagnosis for twenty years? The answer may lie in Qi Space.

In this layer of our reality, the intangible maneuvers in fluid brilliance. To say that everything is energy *here* is somewhat limiting, as everything is energy *everywhere*. We simply forget this when things are solid and visible. In Qi Space, movement is not confined to time and distance. It is a singular, unified existence. The apparent past folds into the apparent future. Physical space collapses upon itself and distance is reduced to an infinitely mutable point. It is here that we encounter Qi. Here, we experience unexplainable phenomenon from healing to spontaneous awareness. It is where we discover our true self.

To *describe* something is to remove it from its essence, says the *Tao Te Ching*. To even attempt to put experiences from Qi Space into words is futile at best. Qi is such a conundrum. Like my experience with students sharing their impression of Qi, we see how impossible it is to use words to convey what we feel—at least in a way that also describes what others are experiencing. It's as if we are describing a dream moments after waking. We all know that strange sensation of watching your memory of a dream event fade faster than you are able to recall it.

The Chinese word *Wuji* (pronounced "woo jee") helps me understand this phenomenon. My teacher Master Duan describes it as "the transition between form and formlessness." Wuji is made up of two Chinese characters, *wu* and *ji*. *Wu* suggests "nothingness" while *ji* refers to "a limit." Think of it as "the limit of nonbeingness." It describes that event horizon where imagination morphs into the tangible, a membrane of probability where matter becomes anti-matter and dreams become solid. As the Chinese language is built on concepts rather than absolutes, a word like Wuji must be seen in a flexible and dynamic manner. Language is one of the many beautiful things about the Chinese culture. Having inherent flexibility and dynamism in a language shows these traits in the thought processes of the people who speak it. Qigong springs from this way of thinking.

Wuji describes Qi Space to me. It is that zone where things are neither matter nor energy. It is a transitional place energetically. Becoming sensitive to this means becoming conscious of the transformative nature of our existence. Through Qigong practice we become conscious participants in our destiny. The Chinese call this *yuan fen*, a concept that goes beyond destiny, fate and even karma. As *yuan fen* includes these ideas, we can see that there is a continuum of energy that ties the past with the future, placing us in a present that stretches in both directions along the time line. Qigong helps us understand that nothing is fixed, as the Tao is an ever-changing flow of energy. So our yuan fen is also flowing, constantly in flux, moving with our very thoughts and actions. As this constant transformative process takes place, our past and future constantly change as well. This may seem a strange concept at first as we are taken to believe that the past is a fixed reality, completed and thus unchangeable. If we understand the Tao, this cannot be an acceptable conclusion. As we flow with the natural way, all in our existence flexes and reforms. Qigong practice awakens us to the fact that even our past can undergo a drastic metamorphosis. When this occurs, the lines of causality are redefined. Past experiences are perceived in a more universal way and with an objective clarity. The perceived present is concurrently objectified and we are released from the perceived past. We must simply allow ourselves to become free of the trappings that bind us to form. As "Dreamtime" describes a malleable reality for the Aboriginal people of Australia, Qi Space assists us in releasing form and becoming the free souls that we truly are.

Entering into our natural state is the gift of Qigong. Reading words like this only serves to trigger our innate sense of this truth. This is all words can do . . . they inspire. The curious thing about the word "inspire" is that its etymology leads us to the Latin word which means "to breathe." This is the fundamental of Qigong play. Learning the breath, following the breath, becoming the breath . . . this is our pathway to understanding. As the *Tao Te Ching* notes, "knowing" is simply collecting facts, "understanding" (the Chinese word is *wu xing*) is experiencing an inner acceptance. I believe that when we have *wu xing* we undergo a transformation. This occurs in Qi Space as it encompasses the body/mind/soul complex. Learning to become sensitive to energetic flux is part of the Qigong experience.

My first formal spiritual and Eastern healing teacher was an eighty-one-year-old doctor named Thane Walker. I studied with him in Hawaii for a couple of years in the mid-1970s. Living in his clinic on the beach was a round-the-clock lesson. The Qigong he taught me was a sedentary one, reflecting his roots in Ch'an/Zen Buddhism. The aim was to release form, to immerse oneself in the universal truth, in nothingness, in Wuji. This was an excursion into Qi Space. What emerged was what he liked to refer to as a *metanoia*, a deep, transformative *wu xing*. Metanoia actually translates as "a change of thinking." We can have a metanoia that awakens us to a long-awaited answer to a puzzling question. We can have a metanoia that is a realization of sorts that sets us on the path of healing—physically and spiritually. "A change of thinking" seems too mental of a definition for me, though. I believe it's more of a restructuring that has taken place in Qi Space.

When the very matrix of Qi Space is affected, corollary changes result in all aspects of our being, manifested in the body/mind/spirit complex. We may see an apparent and obvious change that has taken place, and we assume this is the "result" of the shift. I rather think that *every* aspect of our being has changed in some way—the subtleness may just elude us.

Qigong helps us understand these subtleties. Our daily play helps us appreciate the subtle. We begin to recognize energy shifts even on the most imperceptible levels. This is the path toward understanding the dynamics of Qi. It seems people are either numb to the subtleties of life or overly sensitive. Either state reflects an imbalance. The Tao teaches us to seek balance, to move in a natural and connected way. When we are natural, we shed the illusions of who we feel we must be and begin to act from our heart center, from our true self. When we are connected, we maintain a conscious awareness of Qi Space, of the way Qi swirls around and within us. From this point of view, distinctions between things disappear.

Energetically there is no "you" or "me," no "inside" or "outside," no "good" or "bad." This is the Taoist way. It is not understood from reading a book or reciting scriptures. It is an empirical understanding of the nature of the Universe. The classroom where we can best learn this is in the quiet of our Qigong practice.

It is an issue of trust. Are you courageous enough to trust what you feel and experience during those meditative moments of Qigong practice? Are you courageous enough to trust that Qigong principles are at work in everything that you do? Releasing form, releasing the structure upon which we so fearfully depend is a major step in understanding Qi Space. Thane Walker liked to use the term "parallel universe." It was his metaphor for that potential reality that was possible if we could only release ourselves from the shackles of fear. Once we have experienced this release, we have achieved enough trust to experience the world that has been waiting in a potential state. We can all relate to this when we finally let go of something that held us back. It may have been taking that final step to overcome fear and leap off the high dive at the pool. It may have been mustering the courage to tell a partner what you felt you could never say. These are obvious and maybe simplistic examples of the kind of shifts that take place when we trust and let go of fear. They are actually brief excursions into Qi Space.

Once we can see that this is how the shift takes place on a gross level, we can seek the subtleties of a more refined dance. The quiet of Qigong practice brings us in touch with our breath. Our breath becomes a portal into the trust that is necessary to make the shift into Qi Space. It is a lifelong process. Our nature as humans is a dynamic and shifting one. As humans, our growth occurs in fits and starts; it appears to move backwards and forwards. This is how life looks when you peer at it through the veil of linearity. When you release yourself from the illusion of form, you transcend the limitations of linear thinking. A metanoia of magical quality occurs. Personal growth begins to look like a mesh that extends in infinite directions. It is folded upon itself. We no longer see ourselves moving from here to there, from weak to strong, from bad to good. Growth takes place in a moment. It is actually not related to where you came from or even where you are going. Your existence is complete and perfect in this moment. It is a momentary seeking of freedom, of living from your heart. It is viewing yourself as the infinite and universal creature that you are. A mirror reflecting mirrors. Infinitely connected to a Universe that is infinitely connected.

The Chinese word *wu wei* comes to mind when I think of these things. It can be translated as "effortless effort." I have heard it from teachers on many occasions, from Tai Chi, Kung Fu and Qigong training to philosophical discourses. It connotes the understanding that "no effort" is more effective than effort itself. Its application in martial arts is to use the aggressive force of your opponents to defeat them, guiding them along their own vector into the ground or into a punch. It is the ultimate in flowing with the Tao. Moving with the flux around you rather than bucking the current. Trusting that sometimes moving away from your goal will actually bring you closer to it. Trust. How often we use effort and exhaust ourselves when we simply cannot trust to let go.

A wonderful Zen parable talks of a new and ambitious student who just entered the monastery in Kyoto. After a few days of learning from the great Master of the temple, he went to the front of the other young monks and asked, "How long would it take me to become a Master as great as you?" The Master thought about it and replied, "Twenty years." The young monk, a bit frustrated, asked again, "If I study every day for fifteen hours and without much sleep, how long then?" The Master pondered a little longer and said, "Thirty years." A bit angered, the young monk retorted, "What if I studied harder than all the other monks combined and sacrificed all my interests to show my devotion, how long then?" The great Master pondered a long time for an answer. After taking a sip of tea, he gently replied, "Forty years." With that the young monk stormed out of the temple and was never seen again. The other students were reminded how great their Master truly was.

Wu wei. Approach your Qigong with this spirit and you will be free. Free yourself of expectations, and you will begin your dance into Qi Space. Be gentle with yourself and others. Breathe deep.

Four
Children

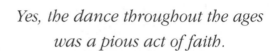

*Yes, the dance throughout the ages
was a pious act of faith.*

Heinrich Heine

I'm continually fascinated by the way children respond to Qigong, whether it's the way they act when they are being treated or the way they follow moves when being taught. Like spiritual Silly Putty, kids are malleable and reflect what they are impressed with. Treat children with Qigong and watch how they react. Sometimes it's with a quiet curiosity as they observe your movements. Sometimes it's from a state of bliss where it seems they have left their young bodies. Sometimes it's with a disinterest that is difficult to accept. But always there is a physiological response that tells you a shift has occurred in their energy. Explain it however you wish. Ultimately children are closer to their natural, spiritual center. Without a massive intellectual, adult construct to burden them, they are pliable and responsive to subtle energetic manipulations. This delicate nature also makes children vulnerable to adult aberrations, so we must be especially cautious around them. Negativity and coarseness that may get filtered out around adults is destructive to children. Knowing this, children can be our best teachers.

Since they respond so fluidly to energetic shifts, children are a great barometer to the state of our Qi. It is a lesson in responsibility for adults. As a conscious participant in the way Qi flows in any given situation, we have the charge of infusing words and actions with life. We have the opportunity to infuse this life we share with positivity, with truth and with compassion. Children respond to this like a well-polished mirror. Observing this is one of the great empirical examples of Qi flow. Try consciously bringing your Qi level up, opening your three *Dan Tians* and *Bai Hui* point [see glossary]. These are akin to your *shakras* or energy centers at various points on your body. To raise your Qi in this way is to bring your focus to your belly, your heart-center and your head. Breathe into these points. Imagine that Qi is gathering and swirling at these centers. Visualize that you are expanding your being to include the children you are with and let it extend beyond them. Bring joy into your heart. Do this around children and watch the difference in the way that they respond to you. Watch how differently they respond to each other in your presence. It's quite amazing.

The fact is, this works on adults as well but at a lower frequency, which sometimes makes it difficult to observe. Change is catalyzed around adults but there are so many conscious and unconscious barriers that reactions can be muted and stifled. To me it just means I have to continue and let go of expectation and the need for any response.

But kids respond and that's the magic of youth. They understand visualization and they trust in magic. They are not so removed from their spirit selves to have forgotten their true nature, even if it is on a deep and unconscious level. One morning while I was in the park studying Qigong and Kung Fu with Master Duan, a group of about twenty little students came up to us. These cute five-year-olds all wore the same yellow caps and scarves so that their watchful teachers could easily identify them in the massive throngs of Chinese pedestrians. I'm sure they were curious to see a big-nosed, blue-eyed foreigner and cautiously came closer to me. I asked a teacher in my broken Mandarin if it was all right to do a little Qigong with them. She agreed and when I turned to get the blessing of Master Duan, he was already sitting on a nearby bench, lighting up his long pipe and smiling with delight. To break the ice, I sang the only children's song I knew in their language, and soon they were all singing along and laughing. After repeating the verses about five times, I felt we had a comfort level and I started to do some Qigong, asking them if they knew what I was doing. They did! Slowly, each of them, all bundled up in winter clothing, followed me with sincerity and focus. It took everything not to laugh at the beauty of the image. Each face was so different, with varying levels of intensity and focus. Watching their little breaths form as mist in the cool morning air was a sight to behold. They followed along intently and were so serious for quite some time. I finally did something funny that I can't remember to bring things to a close and they returned to being children, laughing and playing around. The teachers thanked me and turned to Master Duan to honor him. He got up and started dancing with these little children eighty-five years his junior. China would always remind me to suspend my disbelief and any preconceived notions I may have held about life. This is one of the great lessons of Qigong.

I had a similar experience in Lhasa, Tibet. Doing my morning Qigong in the courtyard outside of the Jhokan Temple was always splendid. The sun rising up behind the temple cast unreal rays through the billows of smoke pouring from the bushels of sage burned as an offering each day. Like China, the concept of personal space in Tibet is about as different from the West as can be possible. Strangers hang on one another to move in and get a closer look at something without even considering it an intrusion. Ego melts into a group consciousness. For the several hundred who gathered around the courtyard to watch me do Qigong, it was a mix of curiosity and entertainment. Since a few in the crowd were able to speak about as much Mandarin as I could, I tried to answer their questions as much as possible. What worked best was showing them a photograph of Master Duan and his wife that I had in my purse. They passed it around, holding it to each of their foreheads and saying something in prayer. This is how they honor everything in this beautiful country. Once the photo returned and I was accepted, the children emerged from the crowd. Teaching these youngsters Qigong was a blast. The adults loved it. Watching a boy giggle from ticklishness as I tried to adjust his arm position got me started laughing. Another boy turned to the crowd with pride showing off the new form he learned. And a sweet little girl seriously watched and repeated my movements, scrunching up her gorgeous little face with each deep breath. It is experience such as this that reminds me of the universal nature of Qigong. It is a language that speaks to the very soul.

I found it curious that in China, Qigong practitioners refer to their daily exercises as "play." It was common to hear someone ask you to come "play" Qigong or Tai Chi with them. What a fun and childlike way to view your health-care!

I met a wonderful woman in Beijing named Lu Yan Fang. She is affectionately known as Engineer Lu and heads up research at the Electro Acoustic Research Laboratory. This facility designs and manufactures high-technology products for the Chinese military and commercial markets. Fifteen years ago, she had a pet project that she wanted to pursue. As a practitioner of Qigong, she attempted to quantify Qi, to isolate it on the audio spectrum. She brought in a wide variety of famous

Qigong Masters from around China for evaluation. She put them in the laboratory's anechoic chamber, a sealed room that is both buffered from any outside sound and padded in a way that prevents any aberrant noise within. Placing a highly sensitive microphone near the *Lao Gong* point in the palm of each Master's hand, Engineer Lu and her staff recorded any emissions that appeared in the audio spectrum. Compared to control subjects who were average, non-Qigong-practicing individuals, Qigong Masters emitted something unique. The scientists eventually isolated this as a random and chaotic wave form that constantly varies between 7.83 and 13.58 hertz. This, they felt, was one component of the elusive force of Qi. Working with Richard Lee and his China Healthways Institute, Engineer Lu developed the QGM CHI Machine to simulate this Qi emission. It is now used by thousands of medical doctors in the United States to treat a variety of ailments from fibromyalgia to sprained ankles.

The interesting part of this story is what Engineer Lu told me about children. She brought in dozens of children and tested them in the same fashion. The curious result was that even though these young subjects never practiced Qigong, they emitted nearly the same frequency and pattern as did the Masters. And like the Masters, they could emit this at will.

I remember that when I was around eight or nine years old, I would lie in my bed and meditate, or at least what I imagined meditation to be. I had read about meditation in some of the esoteric pamphlets that I would get in the mail, you know, that information you could get for free at the back of magazines. My parents always bemoaned the fact that I got more mail than they did. I was curious and wouldn't quit until I got answers to my myriad questions about the nature of existence and our purpose in life. Television shows like *Flipper* and *The Brady Bunch* just didn't make it for me. When I would lie in bed, the palms of my hands would drift together over my navel. I would observe what was happening as if I were across the room or even up on the ceiling looking back at my body. I can remember these experiences like they happened yesterday. I was fascinated by the energy I'd sense between my palms. It was at once within my control and somehow much larger than me. I could feel this force move within the center of my belly and then travel to my palms. Sometimes I would feel as if my whole being was bisected down the middle, literally feeling a partition between these poles. With my conscious breath, they could be brought together and disintegrate into one, unified field of energy.

It became a private game. As I was a child, it was just a fun and a familiar place to enter in between homework and helping around the house. I thought everyone did this sort of thing and just didn't talk about it because it was so obvious. Then I started asking around. It didn't take long to realize that it wasn't what everyone did in their spare time. Maybe the harshest response came from the priests at church that I talked to. When I shared with them my comparisons between the way they held their hands in prayer and what I experienced between my palms in meditation, they came down on me like I was a heretic. Granted, it was still the mid-1960s, but I couldn't help feel that someone was keeping something from me, like a secret that I wasn't being let in on. My young mind thought that they were surely doing a good job at keeping me in the dark. It didn't stop me from my excursions into this energy world though, but it did take another nine years before I met a Master who could help me work with this beautiful and natural Qi flow that I was experiencing. The only one who at least consoled me was a wise old Italian man, my adopted Uncle Mike Napolitano. He treated me, a nine-year-old, like I was an equal. Uncle Mike read a lot of the spiritualist Mary Baker Eddy's work, and that of the Science of Mind organization. He reassured me that it was fine to be experiencing what I was feeling and to just allow it to happen. In time he said, I would understand.

Now that I am an adult, I think about how many youngsters must have experiences such as this. Without a language to attach the words to it, they slowly forget their natural connection to feeling and guiding Qi. The shame is that they are forgetting one of the most powerful tools they have at their disposal to maintain their good health, enhance their intellect and stabilize their emotions. I feel we have a responsibility to children, just as the Chinese take, to help them understand their true nature. To do this is to teach them simple Qigong movement and breathing exercises at an early age, before they forget what they innately know.

Children are our future and I am honored to be working with some wonderful people to help kids discover the wonders of Qigong while they are open and receptive to the magic around them. It reminds each of us to rediscover our youthfulness . . . and Qigong is a fun way to start playing!

Five

Mastery

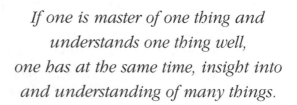

If one is master of one thing and
understands one thing well,
one has at the same time, insight into
and understanding of many things.

Vincent van Gogh

Masters are craftspeople who have excelled to an advanced level. Their experience has taken them through the painful and joyful gauntlet of learning by mistakes and overcoming limits. They have survived this trial by fire. Typically they apprenticed under someone who was their Master, more seasoned in relationship to them at the time. Masters traditionally do not refer to themselves as such; this is an honor bestowed upon them by their students.

In the world of symphonic music, the leader is the maestro, the Master. This person takes on the role of the guide, setting the tempo for the musicians, inspiring with his or her passion. In the world of craft, master artisans cast skillful eyes on the work done by their apprentices. Sometimes only the master artisan's presence and example are necessary to inspire those around them to excel.

In the Taoist tradition, this is the sign of a true Master. True Masters are non-intrusive, saying nothing. Their sheer Qi is enough to infuse a seeker with wisdom. Words and facts bestow only knowledge; Qi conveys wisdom. The *Tao Te Ching*, Taoism's primary text, speaks of how a great leader "does not lead." To be an example in our own life, to live in a virtuous way, to adhere to the principles of truth, this is what it means to be a great leader. The leaders of ancient times, according to this text, were in fact sages, masters of living. They existed in harmonious concert with the Tao.

What does it mean to be a Qigong Master? A Pandora's box of grand proportions is pried open with this question. I have studied with great Masters that were well over ninety years old. Their confidence could only come with the experience they endured, marked by the etchings of time in their faces. A confidence devoid of ego, as they were secure with their true nature. They did not identify with their façade. They could play with their masks, with their various identities, since they were certain that this was not who they were. Their mastery of Qigong was clear since their mastery of life was apparent. In fact, Qigong was no longer a skill to even master. Their life was seen as infinitely expressible. Details and specifics were immaterial. Qigong simply became a convenience, a common language upon which to convey a universal truth. At a certain point of enlightenment, all things so obviously reflect the whole. Qigong becomes a lexicon from which to tell the story of life's fundamental nature. A tree could just as clearly paint this portrait to the enlightened. So could a rock, or a cloud or swimming.

Mastery transmutes complexity into simplicity. It reduces diversity into homogeny. It eliminates waste and fosters efficiency. It makes everything a game. Life is fun. In the heat of the most intense challenge, a Master operates with the same ease and clarity as if taking a warm bath. This release from illusion brings true vision. The illusion that we must somehow act differently in different situations is our downfall. Mastery sees through the illusion of form and allows us to always act from our true nature. When we do act differently, it should be by choice and with the intention to evolve a situation to better teach and reflect its truth.

I've been asked to comment on whether Qigong practitioners should use the title Master or Mentor and whether we even need someone in this role to learn Qigong. I think this is a wonderful exercise, one I believe that lies at the root of Qigong. It touches on the essence of how we view the world. Qigong is in fact the very tool that allows us to alter our world view in hopes of transcending limits and labels such as Master and Mentor.

To me, it shows the clutches of the ego that hamper us to any extent when it comes to the illusion of form.

Qigong provides the gift of fluidity, to flow between definitions and around limitation. This is the essence of the Tao. To know that we are dynamic, changing entities gives us the ultimate freedom of choice. In this choice-filled we can simultaneously be teachers and students, simultaneously reflecting our infinite nature.

Master, mentor? We are at once learning from a teacher and all alone. Find me someone who says they don't learn from a teacher and I'll show you someone who forgot that the trees and mountains around us all are constantly feeding them. Show me someone who says that they can only learn from a teacher and I'll remind that person that it is truly their "teacher within" that translates what they hear into useful information.

The solution for me is to flow with where you are in this moment. Be gentle and sensitive to your needs. You know what you truly need. You will know how to see beyond labels and what you attach to them. Watch the insidious effect of your ego when you are in the presence of a Master. Are you able to be truly humble and open or do you sense competitive reactions emerging in yourself? Are you paying sincere respect or just going through the motions with empty accolades? Our responsibility is to interpret the Universe in a way that most reflects the truth as we know it. Seek beyond the veil and open your searching heart to the truth. Then act from your heart. In this way, you will express your true nature and rarify your Qi to its potential.

I trust that teachers come into our lives when we need

them for transformation. I was just talking to a wonderful young woman who told me that a Qigong Master appeared in her life. She wasn't searching for anyone, not consciously anyway. But then it happened and in a matter of days she found herself immersed in the Qi flow of this powerful woman and watched the confusion of searching for her life's direction dissolve away. Effortlessly, her path was laid before her. She knew in a moment where she had to head. This is one of those incredible phenomena that occurs in the presence of a true Master.

I remember when I was a teenager, and after years of meditation, that I came to the point of realizing I needed a teacher. I sat in the lotus position on a particular boulder in the middle of a creek in Colorado where I was living. I sat and meditated on this boulder day after day. I liked the way the water flowed around it and the sound it made. On the day I had this awakening that I needed a Master to guide me to another level of understanding, a funny event took place. I had the sensation of being very thirsty, mirroring my voracious hunger for understanding, perhaps. A voice said to me, "You will be fed." With that, the sound of the creek got louder and louder. I kept my eyes closed and just grooved with the feeling. Without conscious intent, my right hand fell to my side and I was startled when I felt the cold rush of water. How could the water have risen so high, I thought? My thoughts shifted when I felt something hit my hand. I grabbed at it and opened my eyes. It was an unopened, sixteen-ounce can of Olympia beer! I laughed, opened the can and quenched my thirst as I watched the level of the creek subside to normal. I was immersed in a sense of peace, that all was as it should be. I won't even go into the mysterious events that followed that day, but, suffice it to say, that evening I was introduced to my teacher who guided me as his personal student for the next two years.

When we are ready, we will begin. When our hearts are open, we will receive. Sometimes our teacher is in the form of another person, sometimes our teacher is in the form of a dog. Sometimes we meet a teacher devoid of form. When we are open to learn, we will be taught and healed. Seek quiet . . . listen. You will hear the voice of the dance itself. It lies within your breath.

Six

Healing

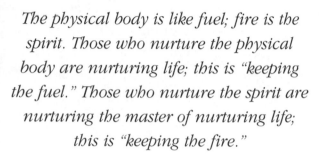

The physical body is like fuel; fire is the spirit. Those who nurture the physical body are nurturing life; this is "keeping the fuel." Those who nurture the spirit are nurturing the master of nurturing life; this is "keeping the fire."

Fu-Kuei-tzu on Chuang Tzu

The very essence of Qigong lies in its healing benefits, whether you wish to heal yourself or someone else. This is because Qigong teaches us to understand Qi. Each time we practice, we learn to become sensitive to the way Qi flows and dances throughout our body. Each conscious move we make during our Qigong play is an opportunity to get in touch with the way Qi courses through our being. As Qi is not confined to the body, learning to sense Qi flow within and around us is a step on the path of grasping the healing potential of Qigong. Learning to sense Qi in others is a major step in developing your own healing abilities.

Over twenty years ago, when I was nineteen, I had a life-threatening experience that transformed my way of thinking. My scars serve as reminders that life is truly magic. I had been studying with my teacher, Thane, in Hawaii for one and a half years at the time, steeped in a round-the-clock learning environment. I was immersed in the study and practice of healing techniques such as Qigong while helping to treat a constant flow of patients at our beachfront clinic and wellness center. On a rare occasion, I had the opportunity to go into Waikiki to take a break from my monastic life. I went to see a performance by a close friend of my teacher's named Richard Ireland. Like my teacher, he was also in his eighties but applied his unique psychic gifts to a very funny "mind reading" show in a big hotel. He was an incredible healer in his own right, using his mental powers to give people answers and suspend their disbelief for long enough to question what they believed to be true.

After the show, I took the long drive home, up over the old Pali Highway and toward the North Shore. Rounding a treacherous cliffside curve, I found myself face to face with an oncoming car at about fifty miles per hour.

In that moment, time stood still. Everything that I had been studying, everything that I knew in the depths of my soul, was called into use in that eternal split second. It was as if life presented the perfect challenge for me to put the theories I knew to practical use. Time passed as if single frames in a movie. In the first frame, I was told that it was "my" accident and that no one else would get hurt. That comforted me. The two cars moved a bit closer. In the second frame, I was reminded of my true nature, that I was not simply a physical body and, as such, I would feel no pain if I remembered this. The two cars moved closer again. The third frame made it clear that this event was necessary for my growth, to help me muster the courage and focus to put metaphysical concepts to utilitarian use. The two cars were nearly touching. The last frame put me at peace, and with a deep breath, connected me to a place of infinite potential. Then there was a loud crash.

The next thing I remember was lying on my back in a bloody pool on the front seat of the car. My white outfit only served to make this more dramatic. Steam spewed from the engine that was now inches from me. Glass shards were everywhere. I was laughing at the beauty of it all. I looked up to see the face of an angel. Well, it wasn't an angel like you may be thinking. It was the woman who was driving behind me just before the accident. Curiously enough, she was a nurse trained in emergency medicine. I began to see what it meant to be in a state of infinite connection. I told her she was beautiful and asked how the people in the other car were. She told me I was in shock and not to worry. I assured her I was fine, though I couldn't see the destruction she was witnessing. I asked again about the others, and she went to check. She returned saying that they were fine, not even a cut on any of the family members. Another assurance confirmed from the vision. I felt no pain—another confirmation. It took hours to cut me out of the remains of my car. I was rushed to the only hospital on that side of Oahu, some forty-five minutes away. I was told I was in bad shape. The long drive gave the hospital time to contact a visiting surgeon, a Dr. Nemechek from San Francisco. He was in town for the week to teach experimental bone-setting techniques. How lucky for me since no one in that hospital was qualified to work on my type of condition. I was on the operating table well until dawn.

Utilizing everything I learned of Qigong, I used my breath to keep my Qi level strong and vibrant while remaining in a relaxed state. I constantly scanned myself from within to make the necessary energetic adjustments. The first day of recovery brought me an uneasy feeling as I sensed in my scan that something was amiss in my right ankle. I couldn't see anything with my eyes as I was in a cast from my waist down and it was hard to move my head to see even if my legs weren't covered. I trusted what I felt and called for the physician. He revealed to me that my ankle was so badly damaged that he had to fuse the joint together. I told him that wouldn't do and that I wanted the option to regain mobility. He told me that anything else would prevent me from ever standing on that leg again. I told him I'd take my chances. He refused. Just then, Thane called from someplace in Ohio where he was teaching. He said he had a dream the night before and "saw" my accident. Amazingly, he tracked me down. I told him of my dilemma with the physician and he agreed with me, saying he "saw" the same thing. As he was also a doctor, he got on the phone with the surgeon who reluctantly agreed to bring me back to the operating room. After another long operation, a couple of surgical pins were installed in my ankle and a frustrated medical team told me point-blank that with this ankle's damaged nerves and my destroyed knee, I'd never walk again. That was not even considering my crushed foot at the end of my other leg.

I applied what I knew over the next six weeks in the hospital, doing various Qigong exercises with breath and visualizing leg movements even though I couldn't physically do them. I received a fresh bunch of flowers from the psychic Richard Ireland every day. He was very upset. He confided in me that he felt like he failed me. How could he predict so many things for strangers in his audience that night and not "see" my accident? This was a great lesson for me. We cannot seek to prevent necessity. If a soul needs to experience certain lessons for its growth, we would only be delaying the inevitable. It seemed only Thane and I saw my accident as a positive event. Within months, Richard shut down his performances and retired to a ranch in Arizona.

By releasing the "form" of what had happened, I was able to truly "see" what was happening. I saw my crippled state more metaphorically than literally. It served to teach me about how I perceived my "movement" through life. My immobility put me face to face with how I was feeling unable to move forward in my life before the accident. Having my feet mangled made me look at my fundamental "under-standing" of the world. It was fabulous and revealing, even if I couldn't even stand up from the wheelchair.

One night, after I had finally been released from the hospital, a group of students and I were sitting around the table at the clinic with Thane. He wanted something from upstairs. As I was his personal aide, he turned to me and asked if I would get it. Everyone chuckled at the humor of the situation. Me, the dutiful protégé who would jump to do what was needed, couldn't even stand. Thane looked very intently at me and asked once again for me to go up and get it. Without missing a beat, I rolled over to the grand staircase, took a deep breath, and visualized my innate perfection and health. I rose and walked up the stairs, struggling a bit to lift the one cast that was still on my right leg. I didn't look back at the table of murmuring students. I kept going in a dreamy effortlessness. I walked into Thane's room to get the object when I saw my reflection in the mirror. It brought me back to this illusory reality and I lost my balance. Arms embraced me and broke my fall. I had not realized that Thane was behind me the whole time. He simply said, "Don't forget this."

My diligent Qigong meditation and visualization helped me to move from a wheelchair to crutches to a cane and finally a freestanding limp. Today, no one detects any vestige of this experience. I play Qigong daily, and it continues to open me. Sometimes the pain returns, but I don't attempt to eliminate it. I listen. I scan my body. I move with the pain. With an open heart, I continue to learn.

As we are unique creatures, each of us senses Qi in our own way. We have our own strengths and tendencies to use the sensory tools we are most familiar with. Some people say they see colors and auras, others hear sounds, and others can get information through touch. It is important to be free to explore your uniqueness. This is the key to releasing form, to understanding that there are infinite ways to perceive the Universe around us.

Qigong is not only a health maintenance or self-healing system. Many practitioners have discovered that they can catalyze the healing process in others. It is fascinating to watch Qigong healers treat patients without ever touching them. Many healers combine their Qigong healing with traditional Chinese massage techniques or even acupuncture. Qigong healing, also known as Medical Qigong, involves the Master or practitioner using Qi to promote healing in their patients. Some Masters believe that it is their own personal Qi that is sent to the patient. This is done by pointing their fingers or passing their hands over the patients. Other Masters, with whom I resonate and trust, do not say they are emitting their personal Qi to the patient, but believe that they are simply channels for the natural flow of Qi. Their Qi is indistinguishable from the Qi of Nature. They put themselves into a focused yet relaxed Qi state as they stand near their sitting or lying patient. The practitioner then moves his or her hands around the patient, conducting universal Qi through their Qi field and into the imbalanced field of the sick person. This hand movement will vary from focusing on the specific area of pain to moving all around the patient's body to settle and balance their Qi. Their hands can be anywhere from a few centimeters to several meters away from the person they are treating. The Master has the experience to "sense" energy imbalance in the patient. They can "see" tumors or hernias that may lie undetected. They can see potential problems that may lead to disease by sensing stagnant, deficient or excessive Qi. The Master will work to rebalance these problem areas by moving their hands in specific ways through the Qi field of their patient. I have seen immediate results and I have seen patients return for several treatments before healing takes place. Once Qi begins to flow smoothly, the symptoms of the illness or trauma will subside.

Learn to trust what you sense. It may not always be what the person you are treating can relate to, and maybe what you sense appears completely off-base. I have found that this is a valid step in the process of discovery. Too many people have unrealistic expectations of themselves. This creates judgments that block their natural abilities to perceive things outside of the realm of the accepted. This kind of intellectualizing prevents you from entering Qi Space. Each time you are gentle with yourself and go with what you feel when attempting to sense the quality and state of Qi in another person, you are honing your skills. Even if you are "wrong," you have allowed your spirit the freedom to express itself. This opens the energetic pathways to go further, to widen your vision and fine tune your sight. It is only through these experiences that you can discover your potential, your innate gift of vision.

This also applies to your own health maintenance and healing process. When we strive for specific answers to "what's wrong," we limit our ability to hear the truth. It's like reducing the flow of a river down to a small straw. The pressure becomes great and virtually nothing gets through. By letting go of trying to get the "right" answer and just letting sensations flow, we begin the true healing process. I have seen that with some clients, their true healing actually lies in the process and not in eliminating their symptoms. Sometimes just releasing their expectations of themselves points them to their fundamental block. This is where their Qi blockage actually resided. Their physical symptoms were triggers and decoys of sorts. They seemed to spontaneously disappear once the real blockage was released. This is a typical example of healing in the context of Qi Space transformations.

This leads to the dance of the healer. It forces us to look with an open heart at what healing really is. Stephen Levine's books and the work of Tibetan Buddhist Pema Chodron go into great depth on this subject. I deeply respect their work and recommend reading them if you are interested in the essence of healing. Unless we can grasp what healing truly is, we will forever be a puppy chasing its tail.

At the heart of healing lies the definition of our identity. Who is it that is healed? My early spiritual and healing training was primarily focused on that *koan*, on that puzzling question. As a teenager I had to make the leap from only intuitively and intellectually knowing that I was an infinitely expressible energy body. My Master had to push my eighteen-year-old ego to the very brink of its grasp on reality so that I could understand with my whole being. This is the battle of the ego versus soul.

Whether the aim of our Qigong practice is personal health maintenance or to heal others, the monster you must face is your ego. I have always seen "ego" and "fear" as interchangeable concepts. Use either in a sentence and they both work. The fear here is that of being a lonely creature, disconnected to all the others. It is the fear that drives you to see every interaction as a confrontation, as a deal, as a transaction where you either win or lose. This adversarial approach to living sets you apart from everyone and everything you encounter. The alternative is to live from your heart-space, to be guided from your soul. You might like to call this your "higher self" or something similar. The name doesn't matter; it's simply that aspect of your being that knows and trusts it is infinitely connected to all you perceive. This is diametrically opposed to the way the ego looks at things.

We are forever frustrated by the Western medical

paradigm that dictates a "healer" and a "to be healed."
The stereotypical image of the egotistical physician con-
jures up a macho, insensitive intellectual whose conde-
scending ways hurt more than help. Granted, things are
changing rapidly. I believe part of this is due to the permission that physicians are getting with the advent of
what we call alternative and complementary medicine, of
which Qigong is a part. It gives sincere individuals the
justification to break the mold and act like humans. It
allows their fear, molded by a devious system, to subside
and let them experiment with moving from their heart-
space. Nurses have been forever challenged by this
dilemma and have become the biggest proponents of
alternative medicine, especially in the area of "healing
touch." Nurses will prove to be the leaders in bringing
Qigong into the hospitals and clinics around the world.
They know the great need patients have for releasing the
ego's clutches. They are the ones who help lessen the
fear and stress that are so destructive to the healing
process. They help patients redefine the way they see
themselves through their compassion. This shift in attitude is necessary for patients to recover quickly. The
pressure that health management organizations have put
on the medical industry by thinking solely from a financial point of view is unconscionable. It ties the hands of
the many physicians who want to do good and give
patients what they require. It breaks the hearts of nurses
who are left helpless. It also seems likely, though, that the
insurance companies will take an active role in exploring

the benefits of Qigong. As the Chinese government is dis-
covering, Qigong is serving to reduce postoperative
recovery time substantially. Its practice by patients is also
reducing their need for medication and this translates to
cost savings across the board.

Our recourse to the current medical situation is to take
personal responsibility for our own health. Qigong is one
way to do this. Coupled with reevaluating our diet and
the stressful lifestyles that we find ourselves in, Qigong is
a powerful tool for healing ourselves in a holistic way.
But what about that ego approach to healing? Unless that
is reconciled, Qigong will never realize its potential for
us.

Two aspects related to the ego are counter to the
essence of true healing: form/expectation and healer versus healed.

Form and expectation come from the belief system that
is strong in the Western world and in fact dominates the
thinking process of most industrialized societies. In
consumer-based economies, form is that substance which
defines reality. It is a materialism that takes us from our
spirit nature and steeps us in a myopia that only puts cre-
dence on things tangible. It is driven by an egocentric
mentality that judges by what things are worth and how
they appear. This way of being only puts trust in things
you can touch and has fixed definitions for each thing. The
world is limited to the physical, and there isn't much room
for the concept of energy or spirit. Coupled with this is the
pressure of expectation. We know that modern advertising

campaigns are predicated on this. People are led to want more "things" and to judge themselves and others by what they possess. Each person becomes endowed with an inherent insecurity of not being, or having, "enough."

This relates to healing in the way we see illness as only the symptoms. The underlying causes are not as important as getting rid of the symptoms. This is called "stuck in form." Pharmaceutical companies play on this and make their fortunes from the quick-fix that people desire to rid themselves of "form" or symptom. When the symptoms reoccur, they purchase more drugs—the loop is endless. The only way to break this vicious cycle is to stop treating only the symptom and to widen our approach to carefully look at the cause of disease. Since taking this approach requires a holistic perspective, which includes diet, lifestyle and emotional state, it is a bit more challenging than just taking a pill. It is, in fact, the only way to break the pattern of limitation dictated by form.

Traditional Chinese Medicine (TCM) is based on searching for the cause of an illness. It treats the whole person, not just the symptom. This tradition comes out of ancient Qigong theories. It is not that the symptom goes without attention, it is that a holistic approach is taken to solve the problem. By taking a step back from "fixing" what is broken, so to speak, we are able to tell why something "broke" in the first place. This approach helps us see what factors contribute to the symptoms that are being exhibited. Thus the "form" is simply a signal for an imbalance that must be uncovered.

Jing, Qi and *Shen* are three very important concepts that can help us gain insight into the ancient ways of looking at balance. Each of these is considered to be a kind of Qi, an aspect of this universal energy.

Jing is thought of as the prenatal Qi. We receive this at birth as it is passed down from our parents. In the West, we can relate to this as the genetic coding imbedded within the chromosomes of the sperm and the egg. In TCM theory, this is only a small aspect of the total concept of Jing. Repercussions that come from the actions of our ancestors also determine the quality of the Jing Qi that we receive at birth. The concept of karma comes into play here. The Chinese have a term called *lun hui* or "return on the wheel." This is the explanation when things from the past find their way into the present. Jing affects our health and vitality in many ways since it is most connected with our sexual energy. Jing is thought by many to reside in the kidneys. This is not to be taken so literally as the organs, but more as the Kidney system which includes the sexual organs. Jing is considered a finite resource in the body. We are born with a certain amount, and it slowly depletes as we age. As the kidneys are thought to affect the ears, it is easy to see why depleted Jing in the elderly often results in the loss of hearing.

Many Qigong exercises help to build the Kidney system and strengthen the Jing. When you practice, it is helpful to keep this concept of Jing in mind. Although traditionally it is believed that focusing your attention and placing your palms a few inches away from the lower

Dan Tian, just below your navel, can help to strengthen Jing Qi, don't worry about the "form" the specific exercise takes; this can be limiting. Focus more on remembering that your intention to build and strengthen Jing is more critical than what movements you are doing. For parents considering having a child, your responsibility is to do everything you can to build your Jing before conception. This, along with strengthening your loving ties to your partner and keeping stress at a minimum, is key to ensuring that the soul you bring into this world will be strong and vital.

Jing is naturally connected to our past. It relates to all that has brought us to this moment. It is our infinite link to the ancient qualities and actions that affect us in this moment.

The next aspect of this universal energy is Qi. This Qi is the energy of our everyday life, created in the laboratory of our body. The alchemy that occurs through the transformation of air, food and experience within our bodies generates Qi. For this reason, we must be conscious of what we breathe, what we eat and what situations we get ourselves into. All these factors must be seen as the raw elements that become the building blocks of Qi. Coupled with this is the state of our body's health. If we are weak or if our immune system is stressed, then our body's ability to generate vital Qi is diminished. It makes us wake up to the importance of each aspect of our lives. To truly be a balanced and vital person, we must take this responsibility.

Qi is the symbol of the present. It awakens us to this very moment. Qi brings everything together to the singularity that is now. Since this Qi is probably the most tangible for people, Qigong practice will show its greatest benefits through the boosting and creation of this. Qigong helps us to be in the moment. Through focused breathing, gentle and synchronous movements, and sincere intention, Qigong can guide us to a noticeable improvement in the quality of our Qi, expressed as good health and a boost in energy. But this is only possible with a conscious effort on our part to honestly look at our diet, where we live and the people with whom we interact. Then we must have the courage to change what is necessary for our well-being.

Shen is the Chinese word for spirit. It is the third aspect of Qi that completes the balance. It affects our moods and our thinking. Shen is the mindstuff that animates our mental and emotional states. It is the Qi that takes us out of our bodies and into the world of imagination. As visualization is critical for balance and advancement, Shen plays an important role in our spiritual development. It awakens us to our soul as this is its essence. Shen fires our creativity and moves us forward. Shen is linked to the Heart system, as the heart represents both the element fire and the emotion joy. An open heart gives us the energy we need to move ahead with our lives.

Shen is therefore associated with the future. It aligns us with our future memories, it connects with the potentiality of our karma that projects into what lies ahead. To rarify our Shen is to open the pathways for what is to come. The traditional way of building Shen is through Qigong exercises that bring focus to the middle *Dan Tian* which is located in the center of the chest, the upper Dan Tian located in the forehead, and to the *Bai Hui* point, located at the crown of the head. Holding the palms a few inches away from these points and visualizing Yang energy from Heaven flowing inward is one the typical ancient techniques to build Shen.

It is important to remember that the definitions for each of these three energies are more metaphorical than literal. Try not to get caught up in specifics. Know that, like a hologram, the whole is reflected in any of the tiniest pieces. In this way, each aspect of Qi overlaps the others. When we perceive life in this way, details inspire and guide us, they don't limit us.

Jing, Qi and Shen. Past, present and future. A beautiful triptych that cleverly brings our life into perspective. To balance these three aspects is to be whole, healthy and fully in the moment. To be too connected to the past prohibits forward motion. To be too much in the present is like running with blinders on. With our heads in the future, we stumble over mistakes that we have not learned from. The past pulls on us with anticipation, worrying about what has already happened (and maybe keeps happening) in our lives. The future tortures us with expectation, always fearful or excited about what is to come. To be fully present is to take into account all of who we are, all that has happened, all that is happening

and all that will happen. The ancient Taoists did not see
time in a linear fashion, for them time folded upon itself.
All points on the timeline coexisted in a singular and unified now. To be in this place is to understand Qigong.
Life becomes a moment of infinite possibility and beauty.

TCM sees all pain and disease as stemming from an
imbalance or blockage of Qi flow. Curiously there are
few psychiatrists in China. A mental or emotional condition is no different from any other imbalance. A patient is
either experiencing excess or deficiency somewhere in
his or her body. Qi is thus blocked somewhere in the
acupuncture meridian network (jing luo) and balance
must be regained. This can be done with herbs and diet,
since the properties of various plants and elements are
known to affect Qi in fascinating and efficient ways.
Balance can be restored with acupuncture, directly working with points along the meridians to promote or ease
Qi flow. It can also be achieved with Qigong, either
through self-practice or by the work of an experienced
practitioner. In any case, the complete person is treated
and brought back into balance, back to a natural state.
The by-product is the relief of the symptom.

I am always pleasantly surprised when someone tells
me that, after a treatment, something that we were not
consciously working on was healed. This is the gift of
releasing ourselves from form. I remember a student in
Malibu who complained of a lower back problem result-
ing from years of sitting at a typewriter editing the local
paper. Her doctor referred her to me to learn Qigong, and

I honor him for his faith. After several weeks of coming to class once or twice a week, she said that her back problem disappeared. More exciting to her and her doctor though was that her painful shoulder, which she had endured for years and never even told me about, felt great. She said she never expected this at all.

Expectation. A funny curse . . . and a wonderful gift to learn from. We sometimes focus so heavily on getting a result that we almost prohibit its achievement. And when we release ourselves from expectation, surprising things happen in our life. I watch health practitioners put all of their attention into solving a patient's specific problem and get so frustrated when they don't witness the "healing." The subtle is forfeited, as the vision is limited to form and expectation. It is our challenge to widen our definition of healing, to see beyond cause and effect. This is how we can begin healing the "whole person." But releasing expectation is no easy task—our societal and family values have impressed it upon us from birth. It takes a courage that must be mustered from deep within us. It takes a trust in our true nature, a trust in the flow of the Tao. It takes that trust that everything is as it should be and that we are active and willing participants in this dance.

This leads to the concept of healer versus healed. I have been fortunate to have many healers, from a wide range of modalities, come to my workshops. A recurring challenge many people experience is that of energy depletion after heavy healing sessions. Practitioners talk of feeling drained by their patients, and they seek ways to replenish their diminished Qi. I have studied with many great Qigong Masters throughout China who are renowned for their healing abilities. I found they have certain qualities and techniques in common with each other. First, they are very conscious of replenishing and enhancing their Qi each time after they treat a patient. They do this with various Qigong techniques, which only take a few minutes. Each method is a typical deep-breathing, slow-movement exercise where they visualize that Qi from Nature is flowing in and through their bodies. Second, they consciously remove any negative Qi that may have attached itself to them. This ranges from washing their hands in cold water to shaking their bodies and "tossing off" bad Qi. I have some very strong opinions about this which I will not go into in this book. Finally, they hold a view that they are not actually "healers" who are healing the patient. Rather, they view themselves as humble conduits for the universal Qi flow. Their balanced Qi catalyzes the imbalance in the patient, and they use their natural ability to channel the unlimited Qi all around them, infusing the ill person with this healing force. They would never say that they are sending *their* Qi to the patient.

I found it curious that many Qigong Masters die at an early age. They are stricken with common diseases, many times the same as those of the patients that they treat. After a little research, I found that these Masters held the view that they believed they were sending their own Qi to their patients. Some Masters would only treat a few patients each day in order to preserve their Qi. Others even charged for the *amount* of Qi that they transmitted! This is what I would refer to as an ego-based healing attitude. Bound by form, we are forced to operate in a finite of limitations. As we are what we believe to be true, we can destroy ourselves by the paradigms we hold.

Moving away from the duality of healer and healed is a step toward freedom and peace. I had one student who was a massage therapist who came to me hoping to solve his problem. It seemed he always acquired the ailment of the person he was working on. I told him that this was quite common, and he was surprised. We worked on various Qi-boosting techniques but mostly worked to shift his attitude away from the healer-duality syndrome. One day he came to me and said he "got" it. A metanoia. When I last saw him, he told me he hadn't taken on anyone's sickness since. Funny how that works.

Massage, or *tui'na* and *an'mo* as it is called in the Mandarin dialect of China, is actually a powerful Qigong technique. Once the principles of Qi are understood, the hands-on approach to healing can be extremely effective. In techniques similar to Shiatsu massage, Qi is "guided" by the practitioner. Blocks in Qi flow are opened and areas of depletion are revitalized. The practitioner focuses Qi into specific acupuncture points through touch. Where the acupuncturist uses a needle, the Qigong practitioner simply points a finger or lays a palm. Palpating the points is a conscious and intentional action to activate Qi flow.

The practitioner acts as a conduit between the Qi of Nature and the patient. The true Qigong physician knows it isn't "their" Qi that's being transmitted, it is a dance with the Universal Qi that moves through them

There are many Qigong techniques used for healing others. That is not the subject of this book—maybe the next one. I've seen many techniques with varying results. One of the more interesting ones is the multi-practitioner system of Master Wan Su Jian of Beijing. His Bagua Xun Dao Gong system uses a minimum of two practitioners at a time and up to six. Practitioners wave their hands around the person being treated and begin a fabulous dance of moving energy. The choreography is carefully followed to get the best results that come from years of research. Qi is first stabilized in the patient and their status is "read." Next, practitioners work to rebalance Qi flow and infuse Qi into the person they are treating. Finally, the patient is rebalanced, energized and grounded. It is a wonderful process to observe and even better to experience. I feel that this offers a great area for research and hope that more groups will explore the potential of this approach.

Like anything in life, Qigong has its charlatans that make outlandish and unfounded healing claims. Taking advantage of people, especially when they are ill, is unconscionable. Please be wary of anyone making statements that don't sit well with you. Keep an open mind, but be cautious. Listen to your inner feelings and try not to succumb to your weakness—the weakness that wants to see you or a loved one healed at any cost. It's a drag that there are healers who prey on this, but they exist in every modality and Qigong is no different. Trust is an important component of the healing process. If you don't trust the practitioner you are working with, the healing equation is handicapped. If you do trust the practitioner, both your Qi fields will be in alignment and you will contribute positively to your own healing. Don't trust far-fetched promises; a true healer will never make them. A good Qigong practitioner should have a working knowledge of Traditional Chinese Medicine, which includes acupuncture, massage and herbs. This is not necessary, but will be a reference point when trying to choose a healer. Mixing one of these modalities with pure energy healing (where the practitioner passes their hands over your body) is a good sign that your best interest is at hand. Some people are truly gifted "energy healers" and have no formal training. A good healer, in any case, should prescribe exercises for you to perform on your own after treatment. This will empower you (and not them) and make you an active participant in the process while prolonging the treatment's benefits.

As there are currently no "licenses" for Qigong practitioners, you must rely on good references and the gut feeling you get when in the practitioner's presence. Take time to talk with them before you commit to a treatment and this will prove very helpful in making your decision. Remain clear in your judgment while staying open to the healing *miracles* that occur every day.

Whatever the system, I believe the most important element is releasing ourselves from the expectations that we hold of what it means to heal. I think healing is unique to each of us and changes depending on where we are emotionally, physically and spiritually. Some people can experience an unexpected emotional healing while never fully eliminating the physical symptoms they originally hoped for. Others may heal their body but never address the spiritual pain, which results in a continued cycle of physical ailments. Then there are the people who never recover from a life-threatening diagnosis but discover that their true healing was completed deep in their soul, and on their deathbed they reveal a clarity of vision and a sense of completeness, love and joy.

Seven
Master Insights . . .

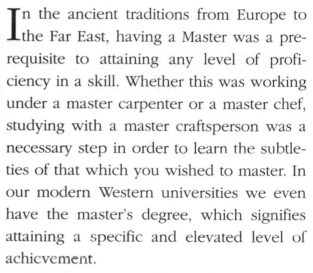

In the ancient traditions from Europe to the Far East, having a Master was a prerequisite to attaining any level of proficiency in a skill. Whether this was working under a master carpenter or a master chef, studying with a master craftsperson was a necessary step in order to learn the subtleties of that which you wished to master. In our modern Western universities we even have the master's degree, which signifies attaining a specific and elevated level of achievement.

China's Qigong and martial arts tradition is similar in many regards. Studying with a Master requires time and dedication since it takes observing the Master in more than just the specific training environment to deeply understand how a skill is to be applied. Spending time with a Master at mealtime or on a walk through the park could sometimes reveal more about a particular theory or system than learning about it directly. This is the gift of training with a Master: watching how experience and absorption of the essence of a skill is reflected in everything they do.

Attaining the level of a Master is not something a person bestows on himself or herself. Typically, the title is given by a student's own Master after it is clear that the student has fully comprehended the teachings. It comes also when it is clear to the Master that the student is dedicated to honoring the teachings and that there is a devotion to fulfilling the role as a teacher.

A Master is at once a teacher and practitioner. Moreover, a Master is an excellent student and remains so throughout his or her life. This sense of humbleness shines strongest in the greatest of Masters. True Qigong mastery reveals that one is on an infinite path of study, participating in an unfolding of the truth and essence of Qigong. This is a lifelong process. A true Master knows there are no absolutes and that discovery continues with each breath. This deep understanding or *wu xing* creates a compassionate tie between teacher and student. It binds souls in a way that reminds us we are on this journey of life together.

The path of study is not a straight line but is, in fact, a circle. True Masters understand in their very being that they are not "ahead" or better than their students. They simply honor that roles and responsibilities are assumed according to what we each must learn most, and how we can best take this into our being. Though we may not always be conscious of or remember that we are participating in an unfolding of the truth of our lives each moment, through the practice of disciplines like Qigong we can become sensitive to the fact that we are exactly where we need to be at each moment. We have everything that we need to live from our hearts and honor our lives—and the lives of those around us.

I asked the Qigong Masters in this chapter to share their personal insights with us. The actual question posed to each of them was the same: *What inspired you to study Qigong and devote your life to teaching and healing . . . and how do you feel people can benefit from this healing modality?*

They represent a wide variety of cultural experiences and backgrounds. They range in age from twenty-three to ninety-two and are both men and women. They all have devoted their lives to teaching and healing. Many of their submissions have had to be translated to English and all are unedited versions of how they chose to answer the same question. Note too that there are different ways of spelling Qigong. For the body of this book, we have adopted the *Qigong* spelling. There are many acceptable ways to spell this word, including *Qi Gong, Chi Kung, qigong, qi gong, Chi Gung.* The spelling for the practice of Tai Chi is a similar case; *Taiji, taiji,* and *Tai Ji* are examples. This comes from the various ways of translating the multitude of Chinese dialects and the interpretations of the translators.

I am honored that these teachers and practitioners have taken the time to speak from their hearts and share their thoughts and feelings on Qigong. May this valuable insight guide you on your journey.

Duan Zhi Liang

Sex: Male
Age: Ninety-two
Home: Beijing, China
Began Studying Qigong: Age five

As my family has always had many doctors in it as far back as we can remember, it was natural that I would be trained at a young age to follow the healing arts. As was tradition, my grandfather, a well-respected physician, was my teacher. My father was a martial artist and was employed as a personal guard for China's last emperor in the Forbidden City. He taught me by example, while my grandfather taught me as a devoted teacher. He passed on our family remedies and Traditional Chinese Medicine techniques, which include Qigong. Our direct lineage of these Qi-enhancing arts goes back some one thousand years. This is when our Christian roots were planted, with the merging of our traditional Chinese philosophies and those of the Nestorian Christians who traveled on what you refer to as the Silk Road.

Qigong began with the first breath of God. This inspiration, this first breath, is the first Qigong. It was the moment nonbeingness made the transition into beingness. This is the power of God. We use the characters *wu* and *ji* to create the word *Wuji*. It can refer to God; it can refer to "endlessness"; it can refer to the "end of non-beingness." It is all these things. This is the essence of Qigong . . . to bring you into the awareness of the infinite nature of your soul.

There are special characteristics of the methods of my family's Wuji Hundun Qigong Kung Fu. These relate to what is practiced by laymen, not the sectarians such as the Buddhist, Taoist or Confucian monks. It is a combination of medical practice, Qigong and the martial arts—all in one body. Wuji Hundun amounts to emptiness. Within its practice, you have no form, no environment, no chaos, no thoughts, no ideas, no ego—no *you* or *me*. It is one, expansive spiritual energy that can guide you. There are no edges, no root or stem. A happy and misty realm of infinite happiness. In embracing the nonpolar, there arise poles. Two forces lead to four environs; four environs give rise to five disciplines; five disciplines is tantamount to six harmonies; six harmonies is the equivalent of eight sides; eight sides equals eight branches; eight branches gives birth to nine chambers. [*This is an ancient description of energy transformation in the creation of the Universe from Wuji or nonpolar, through two forces, Yin and Yang, then descriptions of the Earth through the eight aspects of the Bagua, various sciences and disciplines of life, and ending with nine chambers or the human body—G.G.*]

In practicing Wuji Qigong, exercising is like a great ocean. Be relaxed and feel at peace. The body should swim like a fish, with no weak points nor forceful points.

Neither should there be resistance. Abandon all ideas and thoughts. Minimize one's observations. In this way, repeated exercises will produce real results.

Qigong should teach you to be flexible, not just in your body, but in your spirit. This is why we use the word *hundun* [*chaos—G.G.*] when we teach Qigong. Hundun refers to the nature of this existence; everything is in a state of flux in the material world. To take a rigid stance is to seek an early death. To be inflexible to the change around you is to live in fear. Qigong is a useful tool to improve your flexibility, both mental and physical. To flow with the hundun is to live in a natural way. To make things what they aren't, this is the cause of stress.

When people move too fast or exercise too strenuously, they waste energy. They think they are building energy, but they are wasting energy. They are burning up more Qi than they generate. This leads to bad health. Move slowly, deliberately, breathe deep and with all your skin. In this way you generate more Qi than you lose. The muscles move efficiently and do not burn up all your energy leaving you depleted. Even Tai Chi Chuan can be ineffective. You may move slowly, but it is too rigid, always following the same sequence . . . one, two, three etc. This engages the mind in a fixed way and burns up too much Shen. Mix things up; be free.

The healing benefits of Qigong are equal to its use in battle. Fighting is no different than healing. It is all about directing your Qi. You make the choice of how you use your Qi every day. One minute you heal someone, the next you defend yourself against attack. What's the difference?

Present-day Qigong disciplines are like waves in the world where knowledge is exploding like nuclear fission. Therefore, we have "information theory," "systems theory" and "control or guidance theory"—all coming forth in the field to make their impact and present their challenges. Chinese medicine is also progressing at flying speed. Placed in such floods and torrents of history, we seem to find ourselves in a far-off niche. When the world awakes, people will all realize that the progress in science has wrought on us a common injury in the form of imbalance of nature. Pesticides and pollution of the atmosphere have imperiled human lives. All this worries conscientious scientists to no end. We must work together to reach breakthroughs, especially in life science. What is life science? It is the formulation of the *herbal medicine* of respiration, like some kind of atmospheric engineering that can assist the healing quality of the Universe to reach the respiration mechanism of the body. This will have a positive effect on our goal of healing!

Present-day medical treatment seems inadequate for our suffering public. We are fast approaching the twenty-first century. Mankind is praying for peace in all corners, for bumper crops in all food grains, for tranquility and the conversion of calamity into security. Pray to God for this blessing. May a bountiful and prosperous time await all of us!

We must help each other in this life; there is no other way. Teach those who seek understanding. Learn from those who have experience. Listen to nature all around you and be fed.

Translated by Lui Cho Tuen Lau and Garri Garripoli

Wan Su Jian

Sex: Male
Age: Forty-three
Home: Beijing, China
Began Studying Qigong: Age seven

China's Taoist Qigong Is a Magic Weapon Of Health, Long Life and Peace For All Human Beings!

My Dear Reader,
How are you? Thanks be to God that our destinies have crossed. How wonderful it is to know each other through this book!

Chinese Taoist Qigong medicine has been part of my world since I was very young. As a youth, I began studies in Qigong with my parents. At present, Chinese Taoist Qigong medicine has become the primary focus of research, teaching and treatment at my institute. My heart knows that China's rich five-thousand-year-old cultural history is the result of divine intervention. The Taoist Qigong wisdom from our Chinese ancestors taught us to merge our human and divine spirit. The gift of these teachings was an extraordinary contribution to the health, peace and long life of our Chinese people. Taoist Qigong is the child of the Universe. It is the friend of nature. It is the great law that guides people to return to the essence of their life and remain one with the life forces of the Universe.

Especially, I will never forget how Taoist Qigong saved my life when I faced a catastrophic earthquake. Nature and the are just like my mother. They hold me and protect each day of my life.

Today is a very dangerous time for all sentient life and our home, Mother Earth. As you know, we are stripping the forests from the face of the Earth. We are continually draining the natural resources as oil and coal from her bowels. The consumption of our Earth by draining her natural resources is very dangerous for the future of the good health and peace for all of humanity. For me, I have great faith in the importance of developing Chinese Taoist Qigong theory and practice. I can never dismiss the five thousand years of Chinese culture and wisdom that my parents and my teachers imparted to me. My life is dedicated to improving all people's health and work for peace in the world.

In the past, the current practice was for one Qigong practitioner to treat the patient. The Qi from one physician was sometimes not very strong. The effect was not very dramatic on the patient, when treated by one Qigong physician. I pondered this question: "If he used many people working from many directions, would the effect to the patient be stronger?" I was preoccupied with this question during the day. And to my surprise, one night I had a dream about many army tanks attacking an airplane. By working together, the tanks were able to shoot down the plane. I got very excited about applying this strategy to treatment with Qigong. We used this idea with Ba Gua from Yi Ching to study the effects of direction on the Qigong treatment. Over many years, I researched the integration of the theories and slowly develop Ba Gua Qigong.

May I offer a sincere invitation to all of my American friends to visit our Beijing Traditional Medical Exchange Center.

Sincere best wishes from your Chinese friend,

Qigong Master and Physician Wan Su Jian

Luo You Ming

Sex: Female
Age: Ninety-two
Home: Beijing, China
Began Studying Qigong: Age ten

All my life I did good things and I am happy many students have been able to learn from me. I began studying Qigong and Wushu when I was just a girl, learning from my grandfather. He taught me that the force from the heart can do many things. There are many forces inside us, not only physical strength. I may be ninety-two, but I am very forceful.

You must do good things for the people, nothing bad—this is a socialist country after all. I have been told I have more than five thousand students around the world . . . and more than five million patients. I must be getting old. The most important thing is that you must be honest. You can't only think about money. Patients must pay, but you must get your money from treating people honestly. There are many grades of doctors, some high and some low. I have used my big finger for more than seventy years, it's very important in my healing work. Anywhere in the world did you ever see anyone just use their thumb? If I am invited to America to teach, I only need to bring my thumb!

You must do good for your country, for others; this

keeps you healthy. Some patients are rich and some are poor, but you must treat them all the same way. I'll do anything to help a patient, yet some can be cured and some just can't. Everything I do is for the good of the people.

Shi De Ren

Sex: Male
Age: Sixty-three
Home: Shaolin Temple, Henan Province, China
Began Studying Qigong: Age twenty-one

I came to the Shaolin Temple after graduating from university in 1959. Times were different then and I knew that entering the Temple to devote my energy to Ch'an meditation was what was right for my development. This included Buddhist Qigong practice. The best time to meditate is after 12:00 A.M. We must study Buddhism; the average man thinks of so many things, he must sit and not think of anything else. Forget about inconvenient conditions, just sit . . . don't worry about crossing your legs, just sit. If you're sick, don't think of it or identify with it, sit, meditate, relax, take your mind off the sickness. Become nothingness; here there is no sickness. If you have trouble stilling the mind, repeat "Namu Ami Do Fo." This translates to "I return to unlimited time and space of the Buddha," but don't worry about what it means, just repeat it. When inner and outer are still, you will be free. Buddha was an average man, like us. This inspires me. He was a common man who learned to control time and space. This is Qigong. Buddha is a man, not a spirit. He can show us how to solve our troubles. He was clever enough to get rid of his troublesome desires.

Everything belongs to Qigong. If I return to the natural
time and world, I become free. Just like a point has three
world coordinates, if I am free, I can move into unlimited
time and space. Buddha is a man whose power is unlimited; he learned to control past, present and future. This
is ultimate Qigong. Taoist Qigong may look like this, but
they want to make things still. Buddhist Qigong says all
things have movement. A river continually flows, you
never enter the same river at the same point. Nothing
stops moving. A man can live forever in his mind, but the
body is a shell, it is temporary.

Namu Ami Do Fo.

Kenneth S. Cohen, M.A.

Sex: Male
Age: Forty-six
Home: Colorado, U.S.A.
Began Studying Qigong: Age sixteen

A Spiritual Renaissance:
Reflections on a Qigong Life

It is hard to believe that I ever *began* Qigong—it is so much a part of my life. Nor can I conceive of a time when the practice will end or—God forbid—when the learning will stop. I was first exposed to Chinese culture through a "mistake." In 1968, a friend recommended a book called *Sound and Symbol* by a German musicologist. As I rode home on the subway that afternoon, I realized that in my haste I had mistakenly purchased another book of the same title but by a different author. Instead of a book about music, I found myself reading one of the rarest and finest introductions to the Chinese language, *Sound and Symbol* by Bernhard Karlgren. Before the subway ride had ended, I was hooked. I realized that by studying a truly foreign language I could learn how language and concept influence one's perception of reality. Perhaps I could, in the process, free myself of the preconceptions hidden in my own language, English, and learn to perceive the world silently and thus, more truly.

Within a few months, I began to study the Chinese language and, not long thereafter, Qigong.

As I reflect on this story, I realize that it explains not
only how I began Qigong but why I have continued.
Foreign language study can clear the mind of culture-
bound assumptions. Similarly, Qigong liberates the student from preconceptions held in the body: the immature
and inappropriate strategies for living embodied in posture and breathing. To stand straight is to give up the burden of insecurity. To breathe slowly is to take life as it
comes, without allowing memory or expectation to inter-
fere. As the body becomes quiet, the mind becomes
quiet. The Qi flows not only within the body, but
between oneself and nature. In breathing, the external
world becomes you. Yet you do not own it, you let it go
and return breath to its source—what Chinese people call
the Tao.

I had another beginning, a renaissance of Qi, several
years later. I was teaching my first seminar at a growth
center in Amherst, Massachusetts. One evening, during a
break, I decided to take a walk outside; snow was falling
and hanging heavy on the pine trees. Wouldn't it be wonderful to practice Qigong in this setting? As I began practicing, something very odd happened. Normally, I
experienced Qigong movements as arising from deep
within, seemingly generated by the breath and by the
slow shifting of the weight. But this time *I disappeared;* I
felt that I was not doing Qigong. Rather, the falling snow,
the trees, the air, the ground itself were unfolding

through the various postures. I became a sphere of energy whose center was everywhere. This was a kind of spiritual rebirth in Qigong; I learned that mind and body could become truly empty, that inside and outside could become a unified field of awareness. I cannot claim the experience as my own, because the experience was without "I." But I do know that Qigong has never been the same. Thus, another key to my motivation and, I hope, to your motivation: Practice Qigong to learn that you are part of nature. When you breathe, it is the wisdom of nature that breathes you!

Finally, I have continued practicing because of the dramatic effect Qigong has had on my own health. I was a weak and sickly child and a victim of the poor medical practices of the time. Antibiotics were prescribed for every cold and scratchy throat, leading to a downward spiral of poorer and poorer health. Qigong cured my chronic bronchitis, weak immune system, poor sleep and low energy. I look for ways to bring these same benefits to my students.

I applaud the scientists who are looking for the mechanism of Qigong—how it works—and who are designing the experiments to validate Qigong's efficacy as a form of complementary medicine. Science has already demonstrated Qigong's powerful healing effects on cancer, heart disease and chronic pain. However, people who practice Qigong with an open mind do not need proof to know that it works. They *experience* it. Science has yet to prove that the sun exists. Yet this does not prevent us from enjoying its light and warmth. Yes, trust science. But trust yourself even more.

Effie Poy Yew Chow, Ph.D., R.N., Dipl.Ac. (NACCA), Lic.Ac.

Sex: Female

Age: N/A

Home: San Francisco, California, U.S.A.

Began Studying Qigong: 1962

Qigong is indeed the people's medicine in the twenty-first century, getting them in touch with and taking charge of their own lives for a healthier today and tomorrow. I believe that giving individuals the power to determine and manage their own health and destinies is the secret of true healing. Their minds and bodies are powerful instruments, the ultimate healing machines, and Qigong promotes this.

The year 1962 was a pivotal point in my life. A startling telephone call came from my sister in California to us at home in Duncan, British Columbia. "Father just died from side reactions to his medication!" A self-made lawyer and businessman, only sixty-four, very active, but on medication for Bell's palsy and slight hypertension. He was a good father, so gentle and goodhearted, well-known in Taiwan and the West Coast of Canada and the United States. He had voluntarily helped so many people emigrate from China, giving them a new start in life in America.

The shock threw us in disarray. It couldn't happen to

us! Being a nurse, I had seen other people react to medication, surgery—and yes, even die as a result—but it can't hit my own family. However, it did!

Being Chinese, I had grown up with traditional Chinese medicine and Qigong as part of my cultural heritage. My father and family friends who practiced Qigong and many forms of traditional Chinese medicine had helped so many who were relegated to living with their serious conditions and dying. Like Mr. Wong, who was supposed to die at any moment in the hospital. As a last resort, the physician permitted father and friends to work with him —herbs, nutrition, Qigong, moxibustion, acupuncture. The smell of moxa (like strong marijuana or smoldering fire) permeated the hospital! My father was like the Chinese mayor in Duncan, so it was dispelled with humor rather than ridicule. And, Mr. Wong lived for another fifteen years—a bafflement to the medical staff!

In those days, anything other than mainstream Western medicine was looked upon as weird superstition, almost witchcraft, and ridiculed openly and mercilessly. (Today, that still exists in many places.) So we kept quiet about Chinese medicine and Qigong, and we conformed to Western standards. It was an irony. The Western medicine that I dedicated myself to as my profession had taken my father's life and yet Chinese medicine, which was considered a superstition, had saved many lives that would have died. This didn't make sense!

My mind and my heart were sickened and in a turmoil. What is the truth?

With father's death, I felt a sense of injustice, angry, helpless, frustrated, resentful about the prejudices, all of which was normal for the circumstances. Then I transferred these feelings into a positive energy to search in-depth for that truth, whatever it might be.

I searched intensively for that truth for another ten years. However, it's always an ongoing search, even today. As a nurse exploring my own cultural medicine, I evolved into formal training in Traditional Chinese Medicine (TCM) and Qigong in Canada, Taiwan, Hong Kong, China, the United States, Europe, etc.

More "miracles" like Mr. Wong took place in the tiny offices of my Qigong masters and acupuncturist/Chinese medicine teachers. I saw stroke cases paralyzed for many years and within a few treatments, they could walk with balance. Other "hopeless" serious cases such as people with diabetes, asthma, heart conditions, etc., were getting better. I remember my sense of awe in witnessing so much.

My whole Western training was being thrown into chaos, into question and challenged again.

Then what a lifting of the spirit when, as an apprentice, I started to get surprising results too! I cried joyous tears! Right then I knew I was drawn into something wondrous and powerful in life that most of us had forsaken or never consciously learned.

Each of us is born with this wonderful Qi power or the vital life of all things in the Universe and we are all connected as one with nature. Learning about this Qi, people could have more control of their own lives than they were allowed in the present scheme of things. It is holistic of body, mind and spirit with nature.

I felt my heart open—something happened. I found something that could, in part, soften the cruel way that my father was taken from this earthly realm. I began to understand also that death was not an end of life, but a continuum of the life force in another dimension of life.

I discovered more formally the Qi—the *ad infinitum* vital force of all life in this Universe, and the theories of Qigong and Traditional Chinese Medicine.

I believe that finding the Qi was the beginning of getting closer to the truth. However, it seems that the truth changes as you advance to another level. In the practice of Qigong, you cannot be prejudiced, you must be open-minded, positive, loving and caring. The Qi is universal with no national boundaries. You are me, and I am you, we are indeed one another, so that we must love and respect each other, exist in balance and harmony. It is disharmony that creates envy, hate, greed, illnesses and wars.

Father left two (amongst many) main philosophies to live by: "Take pride in whatever you do and do it to the best of your ability—whether it is cleaning toilets, being a CEO of a major corporation, a doctor, janitor, etc." The other is, "Give silently, but receive loudly." So, I strive for ultimate perfection in my healing skills and skills of life, and very few people know of my pleasures in giving.

The miracles of healing have continued throughout my

thirty years of worldwide experience in almost all conditions of health and illness and for all ages. Now my students witness daily miracles with me as I did with my Masters. Out of my wealth of beautiful experiences, I have created the Chow Integrated Healing System and Chow Qigong by working with the body, mind, spirit, nature and energy concepts of the respected systems of Western medicine, Traditional Chinese Medicine and other complementary medicine. It is captured in my book and video/audiotapes. Many have learned from just that set and have conquered their problems.

My long experience also confirms Qigong is effective for not only healing all conditions, but it is effective for the very acts of daily living. For Qi is the basis of all life. Every culture has an equivalent to Qi.

How diverse are the situations/conditions that Qigong can benefit. Many hundreds of my cases were told that it was hopeless, but with Chow Qigong, life was restored to them. We must keep in sight that life itself is a miracle, which indeed transcends to the miracle of healing.

About four hundred people throughout the world (and growing in numbers) join us in meditation every day at twelve noon, San Francisco time. It is a time to heal and to bring peace to our hearts, to the globe and to the Universe. Please let us know if you do join us.

I travel globally by invitation to see clients, attend keynote conferences and give seminars to upwards of five thousand people, or to provide training, and I love it.

I have now found a beautiful blend: the best of the

West and the best of the East. The East West Academy of
Healing Arts (EWAHA), San Francisco, was set up in 1973
for this purpose. The Qigong Institute-EWAHA was added
in 1988. The World Qigong Federation and the American
Qigong Association were formed by popular request to
serve as a clearinghouse and set policies and guidelines
for practice.

It's been both a painful and joyous search. Every day
my life is filled with wonderment of the miracles that we
can create in this life and help people find again the
miracles in their lives.

My love to you all and I'm prescribing for everyone
eight hugs a day and three big bellyaching laughs a day
to you. Overdosing on these is definitely okay! Please feel
free to contact me.

Jerry Alan Johnson, Ph.D., D.T.C.M., D.M.Q. (China)

Sex: Male
Age: Forty-five
Home: Monterey, California, U.S.A.
Began Studying Qigong: Age eighteen

The Awakening

What first inspired me to investigate Qigong and its energetic applications was an event that occurred in the early 1970s, in Monterey, California. Prior to this event, I was only interested in exploring the martial (fighting) aspects of the Chinese disciplines. At the time, I was studying martial Qigong (body-strengthening exercises and meditations), and Chinese traumatology (bone-setting, herbology, acupressure and Chinese massage). These particular trainings were taught in conjunction with Northern Shaolin System (a combative system of Chinese Gong Fu) that I was learning.

One morning as I arrived early for Shaolin practice, I stumbled upon a startling event that changed my life forever. My teacher had not expected me to show up quite so early, and he was deep into his own training. As I entered the room, I observed my teacher standing in front of a table, a lit candle was burning on the table in front of him. His left hand was placed on his lower Dan Tian (lower abdomen), and his right hand was extended towards the candle flame. I was amazed to see the flame blowing away from his hand. Full of excitement, I exclaimed, "That's incredible!" Turning to look at me, he smiled and said, "No. *This* is incredible." At that moment, the flame stopped bending away from his hand, paused in its natural upright direction, then suddenly began reaching towards my teacher's hand.

I was suddenly stricken by terror, thinking that perhaps there was something Satanic at work, and that maybe my teacher was the "Anti-Christ"! My instructor, sensing my fear, began to laugh and immediately asked me to blow hot air onto my right palm. Next, he asked me to blow cold air onto my right palm. He then began to explain, "The technique that you use to change the temperature of air that you blew on your hand [from hot to cold] requires focused concentration in conjunction with the knowledge of accessing shallow and deep internal air current. I am doing the same thing with my internal Qi through my palm. The candle flame issues Yang or electro-positive energy current. If I issue Yang energy from my hand, the two positive charges will repel each other, causing the flame to move away from my palm. If I change my polarity from Yang to Yin, which is electro-negative energy current, the Yang position of the flame becomes attracted to the Yin current of my hand, therefore drawing the flame towards my palm instead of away from it."

I was in shock over the incident because my existing Christian belief system had taught me that these things were normally either contrived by frauds and charlatans, a form of occult magic, or satanic sorcery. My teacher continued, "Johnson, energy projection is not only experienced through electromagnetic fields, light and sound resonation, but also through the third and fourth dimensions of the time/space continuum. Qi or 'Life-force Energy', is the medium between matter and spirit, and exists in all things. It is considered neither good nor evil, but simply exists to be interacted with."

That particular incident planted a seed, which began to resonate deep within my soul. A personal curiosity continued to grow, inspiring me to persistently search for this ancient knowledge of Chinese energetic practices.

By the mid-1970s, I was interning as an acupuncturist and herbalist in an acupuncture clinic in Monterey, California. The doctor I was interning with also prescribed medical Qigong meditations and exercises in conjunction with the acupuncture treatments and herbal remedies. One patient's response to energetic therapy in particular touched my heart. A man in his late forties had polio for over forty years and could not dress himself without pain so intense that it brought tears to his eyes. After several treatments, his motor-coordination was no better, but the pain had completely disappeared, allowing him the ability to work around the physical impairment. Having trained so diligently in the martial arts, learning how to inflict pain, I was now awakened to the boundless possibilities of the healing arts, learning to help ease pain and suffering.

As my quest for knowledge continued to grow, the search naturally led me to a more intense study of the non-martial side of Qigong. Since that time, I have extensively studied many disciplines of Chinese energetic medicine, including: Chinese energetic anatomy and physiology; energetic diagnosis and symptomology; energetic psychology; Qigong pathology; advanced medical Qigong therapeutic modalities; advanced Chinese traumatology (psychophysical integrational therapy) and tissue regulation (neuro-muscular therapy); and advanced visceral manipulation.

This quest for knowledge has led me to understand that energy is inherent in the living human body, and the human body is sustained by energy. In the spiritual overview of Chinese Qigong doctors, all things in nature, and in fact, all things in the Universe, are woven from the same fabric. Quite literally, we are all symbiotically one with the Universe through this system of Qi (or life energy force). The word *Gong*, which translates to skill, describes specific techniques that utilize the knowledge of the body's energy.

Through observation and study, Chinese Qigong Masters discovered that each organ in the human body has a different function and a different speed of energy interaction or vibration. By tracing the pathways Qi takes through each organ, and observing the outcome of cause and effect within the various function(s) in the body, the basic theories of Traditional Chinese Medicine (TCM) were developed. A comprehensive system of specific

methods and exercises were perfected, and they have
been successfully utilized in clinical application in China
for thousands of years.

Through the study of Qigong, anyone wishing to cultivate awareness of the energy vibrations and their unique
individual pathways can learn how to influence and even
control them. Qigong doctors use these skills in healing,
strengthening the immune system and aiding the functioning of various organ systems within their patients'
bodies. According to estimates, in Beijing alone, more
than 1.3 million people practice some form of Qigong
every day, and in China as a whole, approximately eighty
million people practice Qigong.

Traditional Chinese medicine maintains that when living things start to lose their Qi, they lose their vitality. An
ancient Chinese saying states, "Life comes into beginning
because Qi is amassed; when Qi is scattered, the person
dies."

While the concept of Qi may seem complicated, it is
actually very simplistic and logical in the progression of
matter to energy, and energy to spirit. Qi is simply the
medium between matter and spirit. Once we become
aware of the tangible, existing reality of Qi, it is easily
recognized.

The purpose of treatment with medical Qigong is to
release and purge strong toxic-energy flows that are literally trapped in the body's tissues. When we hold back
our feelings, we block our natural Qi flow, which creates
stagnant pools of toxic energy within our body. For the

healing process to work there can be no separation between body, mind, emotion and spirit. All must be in balance to maintain a healthy body. In medical Qigong procedures, the doctor trains the patient to focus attention equally on their physical, mental, emotional and spiritual functions.

There are many styles of medical Qigong training, most of which involve all of the individual's physical senses. Specific application is focused on breathing, hearing, visualization, concentration, muscle relaxation, massage and movement to develop and control the body's intrinsic energy, which promotes overall health and aids in preventing disease.

Through years of clinical application, I found the use of medical Qigong therapy extremely effective, and in 1993, decided to further my studies of energetic medicine in China. While training in China, I went before several medical review boards and became the first foreigner allowed to treat patients in the medical Qigong clinic at the Xi Yuan Hospital of Traditional Chinese Medicine in Beijing (the hospital featured in Bill Moyers's special on "Healing and the Mind"). There, I interned as a doctor of advanced medical Qigong therapy, specializing in the treatment of cysts, tumors and kidney dysfunctions.

Over the years, I have trained in several of China's prominent medical Qigong hospitals and clinics, and was able to observe, as well as treat, hundreds if not thousands of patients with medical Qigong therapy. Through these experiences, I began to fully comprehend the healing potential of this unique style of energetic medicine. I observed the effects of treating many patients with certain medical Qigong techniques that were very effective in dissolving specific types of cysts and tumors, as well as enhancing the patient's immune system.

Noting that medical Qigong therapy (which is older than acupuncture) is not a "new" system of healing, but thousands of years old, and realizing the validity of its functional practice, I have found that more people are becoming open to its health and healing benefits. Studying medical Qigong requires not only comprehending the immeasurable wisdom gathered for medical, martial and spiritual development, but also studying the ancient Chinese culture inherent within these systems.

Zhi Chen Guo

Sex: Male
Age: Fifty-six
Home: Heibei Province, China
Began Studying Qigong: Age twenty-two

The survival and existence of human beings depends upon establishing a harmonious relationship with nature and as such must follow the changes in nature. The quality of our natural environments affects the life and health of human beings. Therefore, humanity must investigate nature's abilities to survive and thrive and utilize that information to create natural treatments which then lead us on our search for the source of life.

Zhi Neng Medical Science (Mind and Energy Developments Medical Science) is my masterpiece and is a result of my forty years in personal practice. My observations of clinical healings led me to develop and apply the human subconscious to the synthesis of Chinese and Western medicines. This merger with the extraordinary superpowers of the mind into one unit became the basis of rules of research that led me to comprehend the rules of matter, energies and messages that exist between the human body and nature. This depth of understanding into these relationships became this brand-new medical science with its high degree of complexity which cures diseases, improves health and develops intelligence.

Honestly speaking, this is a collective and multi-functional mind and energy development science series, which I hope will one day be one of the replacements to the traditional Eastern and Western medicines.

The theories of Zhi Neng Medical Science are based on the relationships between matters, energies and messages and the theories of the movement of cells; fields and field images; and space and energy movements utilizing the human subconscious to research biological, pathological and other fast clinical judgment and healing methods.

Through the observations of the field shapes and field images of the human body, listening to the changes of field sounds and reception, and observing the messages sent out by the human body, I witnessed the disclosure of the human body's deepest secrets. These secrets and the wonders of nature indicate the content and reality of Qigong sciences.

Zhi Neng Medical Science developed into a series of special healing methods which include hand gestures, self-healing methods, subconscious-message methods, group fields healing methods, herbal wine-burning healing methods and the establishment of new herbal theories through the application of the human body's subconscious, all of which led to the discovery of the uses of the functional rules of Chinese herbs in human bodies.

Pinpointing the essence of the theories of Zhi Neng finally formed the Theories of Subconscious, *Shang Han*. Breaking through the rules of the herbal applications of traditional herbalists resulted in the healing principles of

functional transfers to cure diseases which utilize messages of the human body and Chinese herbs. Written pre-
scriptions, clinical judgments and healings are all done at
the same time. This demonstrates that the theory of Zhi
Neng Medical Science combines the essence of modern
medicine and traditional medicine with noteworthy new
discoveries, creations and research results.

After large numbers of clinical applications, we recognized the causes of several world-renowned diseases that
afflict large numbers of the world's populations. We
observed cancers caused by problems of dual pressures
within and outside the cells; drug addiction caused by the
loosening and tightening of cells; AIDS caused by the
problems of cell penetration. We have also been able to
make clinical judgments and healing breakthroughs in
various early and mid-stage cancers.

Following the positive developments of Zhi Neng
Medical Science, we have earned admirers and patients
from inland and abroad who flock to us and are benefiting
in countless numbers. Our principles of fact-finding, seeing
to believe and the standards of truth which are the foundation of the practice of Zhi Neng Medical Science have
enabled us to apply these benefits to healing, industrial and
agricultural research and research into new frontiers.

Since science and medical science are still developing
and advancing, my hope and desire is that Zhi Neng
Medical Science will create a new era in human medical
science as we enter the millennium. It is my fervent
prayer that we will all join hands and work for the

increased visibility of this science so that we can make even bigger contributions to the health of all the peoples of the world.

Zhi Gang Sha

Sex: Male
Age: Forty-one
Home: Toronto, Ontario, Canada
Began Studying Qigong: Age ten

As a child, I was very sick. I was tired all the time, I had no strength or energy and was not able to play with other children. I was lonely and my life had no joy. My father tells me that as a result of allergies, I was given penicillin and developed an allergic reaction to that drug which caused me to go into a coma. My family feared I was dead as I had no color and was ice cold. An acupuncturist was called who inserted one needle beneath my nose which caused me to immediately "come alive." I now believe this incident contributed to my desire to be a healer.

At age six, I experienced a second miracle. During an outing with my parents, we went to the park. I was immediately attracted to what my young eyes thought of as an old man who had more strength and energy than I did at age six. He was practicing Tai Chi. I felt compelled to approach him and remember saying "Grandfather, I want to learn from you, I love this dearly." The Master took an instant liking to me and had me summon my parents. With their permission and in what seemed like an instant, I became a serious student of this renowned Tai

Chi Master. Within four years, I regained my strength, energy, stamina and health and was practicing Tai Chi from two to three hours daily. At ten years of age, I started my Qigong training with this and other Masters in the region around my home of Xi'an, China.

Throughout my lifetime, I have also been a serious student of I Ching and Feng Shui. I have had the privilege of studying with Professor Liu Da Jun of Shan Dong University in China and renowned Buddhist Master Wuyi of Taiwan. Since 1986, I have studied with Master Zhi Chen Guo, the founder of Zhi Neng Medical Science. I am his adopted son and function as his world representative charged with bringing this subconscious science to all the peoples of the world.

I attended Xi'an Medical University and studied Western medicine and obtained my M.D. degree in 1983. Combined with my training in the ancient healing arts, I became the Qigong and acupuncture instructor at the International Acupuncture and Qigong Training Center in Beijing. I provided international physicians who were affiliated with the World Health Organization with an increased understanding of the principles and uses of these healing arts—after all, I am living proof they work! I then taught a similar program in Manila, Philippines.

Since 1990, I have been practicing and teaching Zhi Neng Medicine which combines the best of the West with Traditional Chinese Medicine, Qigong and spiritual studies. I have been privileged to train thousands of students worldwide to heal themselves with Zhi Neng Medicine.

Many of my patients experienced chronic pain and fatigue and suffered emotionally and spiritually. The techniques they learned enabled them to recover their good health and joy for life. I am deeply moved and encouraged each time I witness the benefits of these healing and energy-boosting techniques. I am also committed to teaching Soul Study, which includes soul development, communications and healing to wider and larger audiences in the West, since in China millions of people have benefited from these practices.

Lily Sioux

Sex: Female
Age: N/A
Home: Honolulu, Hawaii, U.S.A.
Began Studying Qigong: Childhood

Daily I practice Chi Kung, giving me the feeling of peace. Every day it gives me energy, it channels my tranquility, it nourishes my spirit, and it opens my psychic power. It allows me to be what I am. Not only to date, but I know it will also keep me going in the future.

It connects me with the Earth Mother. Chi Kung makes me feel light and it gives me a flowing rhythm like in music, dancing with my spirit. This practice makes it easy for me to speak with God.

It accesses my mysterious celestial connection. The gentle silken thread of terrestrial breathing opens my third eye. It centers my focus and I gain wisdom. I experience the presence of God. She blesses me and gives me good fortune, good health and settles my roots.

My life is based on the smooth and slow breath of inhalation and the gentle control of small amounts of exhalation for the desire of longevity. The celestial and terrestrial breaths are united in my field of immortality. Each celestial breath raises me closer to lightness, and each terrestrial breath pulls me closer to grounding.

Chi Kung enlightens my path of life. It provides

awareness of the past, present and the future. It gives me a sense of the meaning in life. Being grounded enables me to focus on my life root, and I rise above all matters. It crystallizes my mind, it's always clear. This in turn nourishes my memories.

Chi Kung is my life philosophy, and the quality of my life depends upon it. Nothing can be more satisfying or more fun. And doing it keeps my soul, spirit, body and mind alive. When the Chi is processed through breathing, the merit of Kung is manufacturing the unseen life essence, and then this essence is preserved in my mind, body and spirit.

All of the above benefits are the reasons Chi Kung is part of my life. I suspect thousands of others reap the same benefits from regularly practicing this art.

Roger Jahnke, O.M.D.
Sex: Male
Age: Fifty-two
Home: Santa Barbara, California, U.S.A.
Began Studying Qigong: Age nine

My Qigong History

My first impressions of practices or methods that support us in deepening our understanding, enhancing health and accessing spirit came from my grandmother. It is fitting, given Qigong is often passed from the grandparents to young children. She was very moved by spirit and by the practical application of nutrition, rest, herbs, honesty and fun to create both spiritual calm and vital physical health. I remember, as a very young child, her giving me herbal concoctions, applying simple massage and suggesting that I deepen my breath to seek a state of relaxation and meditation.

So when I discovered Taiji and Yoga in my late teens, in Cincinnati, Ohio, I already had a fairly rich exposure to the purposeful altering of my inner state. One of my grandmother's favorite teachers, outside of her Catholic adoration of Jesus Christ and the Blessed Virgin Mary, was Emil Schmidt, the pastor of a small church named The Universal Brotherhood of the Cosmic Age. After my grandmother's death, I embraced Dr. Schmidt as my own teacher for a while in 1966. He taught me to meditate, to do energy healing and work with spiritual information transference from the Rosicrucian Tradition, which was called "light delivery."

Eventually, when I committed to becoming a doctor of traditional Chinese medicine, I was already immersed in the marvel of Qigong from non-Chinese sources. It was easy, then, to fall into the embracing arms of the profound and ancient arts of energy management and aligning with Tao (Dao). Transferring my earlier skills to the Chinese Qigong context was no labor. Rather, it was an inspiration to expand to inner alchemy, elixir thinking and the quest to understand and attain immortality.

My greatest personal revelation about Qigong came in two pieces. First, when Taoist Master Chang Yi Xiang (Dr. Lily Sioux) accepted me as a student at the Tai Hsuan School of Taoist Arts to study medicine she rearranged my world view by revealing that Chinese medicine did not create Qigong, rather Qigong created Chinese medicine. She made it clear that the most profound healing resource circulates naturally through the body and that Qigong was the method that the Chinese used to discover, understand, nourish and maximize the Qi. Second, I was astounded to realize that I could literally feel the presence of this marvelous elixir energy when I turned my attention to the practice of Qigong.

My greatest revelation about Qigong for others came after several years in the clinical practice of Chinese medicine. Patients kept asking me, "Doctor, is there medicine in the acupuncture needle?" After all, most people in America believe that medicine comes from doctors, frequently through the injection needle. Then I would say, "No, there is no medicine in the acupuncture needle, it is very slender." The next question was clearly a turning point in many people's lives, "Well, then, where is the medicine?"

In Chinese medicine, the most important healing resource is produced within the human body from the natural interaction of Yin (Earth, food and physiology) and Yang (Heaven, air and philosophy). The acupuncture needle assists in balancing directing, refining and enhancing these marvelous inner healing resources.

Finally, after years of personal practice, it settled in through my Germanic Cincinnati heritage that the most profound medicine is really within us. With acupuncture, a doctor is required to give the treatment; with Qigong you balance, direct, refine and enhance the Qi for yourself. For me, this was a remarkable breakthrough, it completed the altering of my world view in around 1978. In China, however, this has been common knowledge for thousands of years.

From then on, my greatest and most compelling interest in Chinese medicine was Qigong. Although I'd been practicing Taiji for over ten years, this was an immense personal and professional revelation—people can heal themselves by learning to circulate and maximize their own Qi—and it is free. This information is not complex or esoteric, average people can learn these ideas and

even share them with their family, friends and co-
workers. The transformation in health care that is so necessary will not come from doctors or politicians—it will
come from the people.

Then, to be sure that all of this was accurate, I traveled
to China five times and visited the public parks, the hospitals, the Qigong institutes, the temples and sacred sites.
Seeing thousands and thousands of people in the parks
(knowing that 100 million people practice Qigong every
day [*this number is one of the current estimates—G.G.*])
was like touching the garment of truth and drinking from
the fountain of original wisdom. Receiving instruction at
Shaolin Temple (Song Mountains), White Cloud Temple
(Beijing), the Qigong Institutes in Beijing, Shanghai and
Guanzhou, and being immersed in the alchemy lineage
of immortality Master Ge Hong in Hangzhou (and the
other great inner elixir [*nei dan*] alchemists) has left me
completely surrendered to Qigong.

My Work Today

Drunk on Qi and addicted to the cultivation of universal energy and spirit within me, I am basically a servant
of Tao. The foundation of my work is to introduce people
to Qigong, to assist those who wish to deepen their practice and nourish the outcome of peace within and among
all beings. Qigong for healing, Qigong for health
enhancement—these are not ends in themselves. Rather

they are means or pathways to the more essential and more supreme human experience—awakening to and merging with Tao, Dharma, Heaven on Earth and the unified field of all essences, things and beings.

My calling now, as a doctor, is to empower people to heal themselves by connecting personally and directly to pure and rich universal essence—the healer within. For those who come for treatment, those who seek instruction, those who use my books and even those who come to lectures, the goal is always the same—to foster direct and personal access to the invisible unifying force that causes life, holds the planets in their places in the heavens and heals suffering.

Asked to distill into one statement, I would say, "Cultivate through Qigong practice to learn the one thing, that when it is known, contains all things worth knowing. Cultivate through Qigong toward the highest, most sublime value—through your practice, import cosmic virtue and universal peace into the human field. This method promises to heal the world and all beings, which automatically will help to heal each individual and their loved ones."

Lao-tzu has said, "Use your own light (radiance, essence, spirit) to return to the source of all light, this is the practice of eternity." When our Qigong is this highly refined, it is less focused on personal pain and ills. Not only do we access healing for ourselves, but we are purposefully supporting the healing of others as well, with no additional effort.

The teaching of my grandmother's Catholic/Rosicrucian Qigong is not so different from that which I have learned from the great healers and monks in China. We study the great Masters Jesus, Mary, Lao-tzu, Buddha, Quan Yin and all of our most revered teachers who have experienced direct revelation to find our own path to direct personal revelation.

Some Concluding Thoughts: Masters, Teachers, Mentors, Facilitators

Some Qigong teachers are looking for students. I do not believe in this. Instead, I am looking for teachers, people who are so inspired by Qigong that they access the simple truth about healing and empowerment and then pass it on to others. I believe an immense wave of Qigong will carry millions and millions of people to higher levels of health, personal performance and peace. Many of the teachers will be nurses, retired doctors, schoolteachers and other citizens who elect to donate their time to strengthening and empowering their community.

Some Qigong teachers aspire to be revered as masters. I, personally, am not moved by this. Instead, I hope to be seen as a mentor, someone who fosters individuals or groups to access their own power and wisdom and to make their own direct connection with universal resource.

Some Qigong proponents insist that one could get hurt without a Master teacher. I humbly and respectfully debate this. I believe that the Qi itself is the greatest teacher and that the most profound source of information is one's own personal practice. The great masters will guide and assist. My own, most-honored teachers have said, and I fully agree, that it is an illusion and a distraction to consider that the only safe pathway into Qigong, Original Cause and the Mystery, is through a relationship with a singular Master. I do not note this as a truth; it is noted as an opinion.

Some Qigong Masters claim that they cause miracles to occur. While I do not debate this possibility, I personally am committed to supporting people to access their own miracles. I have been blessed to be present when Qigong miracles have come to pass, but would not claim to have caused them. Some Qigong Masters claim to accumulate Qi and then project it to another to heal them. Qi projection is possible either as a gift or through vigilant practice. The "light delivery" method from Dr. Schmidt, modified through many learning relationships with Qigong master teachers, has made that clear to me. However, I personally feel it is a distraction from a higher truth when people search for someone to heal them, when it is their highest destiny to be able to open to and receive the universal Qi personally, on their own, through personal practice. When people learn that the Qi comes from another person, it is hard for them to learn that they can have direct personal access.

So, because of these things, it is not so likely that I will create a large following of devoted students, refer to myself as a master or be acclaimed as a miracle healer. I am content to teach people to access their own direct connection to universal resource and inspire them to share Qigong with others.

Qigong (Chi Kung) Poem

Merging with the World

The gate to penetrating the mysteries of the
is opening within you.
Relax the breath,
and attend mindfully to the gathering of vital and light resources.
Purposefully compound, constitute and circulate, the most profound
    elixir
within the alchemical vessel of yourself.
From Yin, our Mother, the Earth
gather and circulate the water of rain, river and sea
along with clay, sand, soil and rock
to sustain and enhance your substance.
From Yang, Heaven, our Father
gather and circulate the breath of air, wind and storm
along with fire of volcano, stars and sun
to sustain and refine your spirit.
Draw upon these equally,
in balance, through the entry gates, transformative passages and
    uniting places
within your local self.
Direct supreme elixir within you
to awaken, activate, nourish, cultivate and refine

healing and empowerment within your body.
Allow the soft radiance of celestial influence
to bathe and purify your soul.
With gentle, quiet intention
surrender to the impulses that naturally arise.
Notice that your arms have transformed
into the graceful white feathered crane's wings.
Notice that the soaring dragon's essence elixir
transmutes the intelligence of your mind's eye
and the wisdom of your own heart.
Notice that the brilliant colors at the horizon
where the sun will soon emerge from the sea
are woven into the blanket that rests softly upon your shoulders.

Roger Jahnke, O.M.D.

Maria Qinyin

Sex: Female
Age: N/A
Home: Cupertino, California
Began Studying Qigong: Age three

I'm a Qigong master, and I founded my version of Qigong—Qin-Way to Health and Sublimation (Q-WHS). Although many people in China and America have learned and benefited from my Qigong, originally my dreams in my childhood were to be an artist, novelist, astronomer or scientist such as Madame Curie. Never had I thought of being a Qigong master and sustaining so much hardship.

I was weak when I was born. At the age of three, my maternal grandmother started to teach me meditation. Among many kids in my big family (including some relatives), I was the only one who could easily quiet down and sit in a full lotus position. My hometown in Southern China, Han Zhou, is a beautiful and historic city. But its climate is often cloudy and damp. One day, when I was playing, I accidentally found out that when I was freed of any random thoughts and called sincerely in the direction of the sun, it soon came out and shined brightly with the sky covered by splendid rays. That year, I was still in my early teens.

From high school through university, I was deeply

occupied by some questions in my mind and tried to find answers beyond textbooks. During a winter break, I went to one of the four most famous Buddhist temples in China——Nan Hai Pu Tuo, which is not far from Han Zhou, and met with my mentor, Abbot Huikong, who let me understand the real nature of Qigong. She taught me some invaluable secret exercises and true methods. During this period of time, I gradually came to understand the renowned Chinese philosophy of "unity of human with Universe." From what Abbot Huikong and later some other grandmasters taught me and my own practice of "dispelling the clouds and seeing the sun," I was fully convinced of this ancient philosophy of "unity of human with Universe" and its epochal meaning for the well-being of mankind.

After I graduated from Zhejiang University, I became a faculty member in the department of philosophy at the same university. In the meantime, I was often invited by the Chinese Qigong Research Society and the Chinese Somatic Science Association to give presentations and workshops. Increasingly, I was attracted to these presentations and workshops instead of my normal teaching job at the department. In my presentations, I not only gave my audience some knowledge of Qigong but also taught them some simple methods benefiting their health. Sometimes, after these presentations, I received joyful phone calls from people reporting on the alleviation of and even complete recovery from their diseases. These moments were the happiest times in my life. In

Beijing, one attendant told me that his diabetes recovered from four "+" to only one "+" at the second day following my presentation. Another attendant with leukemia realized energized fasting continuously for seventeen days after my presentation and fully recovered after discharging some foul-smelling feces accumulated in his bowels.

Finally I decided to say good-bye to my normal academic career and founded a small Qigong college in 1991 by myself in southern Zhejiang Province, China, the Modern Purple Bamboo Qigong College. Dedicated to some ancient and brilliant methods of natural healing, its spectacular effects soon drew significant regional attention. The then-president of the Chinese Qigong Research Society, a most authoritative and official Qigong organization in China, Mr. Zhenhuan Zhang strongly endorsed my Qigong and encouraged me to promote it on a national scale.

However, in the process of my teaching Qigong, I acutely felt that traditional Qigong, although excellent, was still too complicated and sometimes obscure and therefore not easy for modern people to practice and derive health benefits from in a reasonably short period of time.

I made another big decision in my life. I temporarily closed the Qigong college and started to search all over China for some legendary true Masters hidden around the countryside throughout China. After enduring much hardship and being genuinely instructed by some highly qualified hermits, and repeated exploration and experimentation, I realized that Qigong should not focus solely on training the Qi. Actually, it should also emphasize how to efficiently utilize the Qi to achieve health benefits—human detoxification, or in other words, removing toxins from human body. An effective combination of energy infusion and human detoxification can yield a much more satisfactory outcome with less effort. Besides this, I also established some other important Qigong theories and practice that helped to successfully streamline traditional Qigong into a set of simple, clear, and more powerful Qigong exercises—Qin-Way to Health and Sublimation (Q-WHS).

In Beijing, people benefiting from Q-WHS ranged from high-ranking officials and university professors to illiterate common civilians. International tourists were also attracted to my Qigong class. Q-WHS's fame soon spread and culminated in its recognition as one of the most recommended versions of Qigong by the Chinese government in early 1997 at the First National Conference of Public Health and Qigong.

Now I have successfully held several "energized fasting and Qigong retreat" sessions in Northern California, America, with the purpose of fundamentally and thoroughly curing chronic and difficult diseases and significantly increasing the energy level. I had various types of Qigong classes in Beijing, but why do I only hold a special "energized fasting and Qigong retreat" session in America for the present time? One important point is the difference in cultural background. The retreat is especially helpful for Americans who do not have much knowledge of Qigong or even Chinese culture and those who do not believe in Qigong. In my sessions, I often perform an interesting experiment of twisting a steel spoon to show my students of the existence of invisible energy—the Qi. The spoon, impossible to be twisted even by strong young men, became very soft in my hands.

In the retreat, participants can open up their acupuncture points and energy channels and connect them with high energy in the shortest time possible. Under the condition of acquiring an enormous amount of real Qi, every attendant (even those who have not been exposed to Qigong practice before) is able to achieve an advanced Qigong state—energized fasting, that is "too Qi-filled to eat." They were not hungry at all with no food and still had high spirit during in a few days. It has been proven that energized fasting can greatly facilitate various methods for human detoxification, an essential part of the healing process. One participant "perspired the largest amount of sweat since she first came to America," another discharged urine twenty-nine times during two days, and many celebrated in removing stinking stool out of their bodies.

Therefore, it's understandable the miraculous healing effects that these retreats have achieved. On average, obese people lost from eight to eighteen pounds within six days and many looked ten years younger after attending my retreat sessions. An American lady wrote about her experience form during the retreat, "I had no coffee and no food. I did not get a migraine — I always get bad headaches when I don't have coffee. And all day I was not hungry with no food. . . . So far, I lost eight pounds and feel wonderful, even my boyfriend said that my eyes were so green."

Until now, according to incomplete statistics, diseases that have been successfully healed or greatly alleviated in Q-WHS's Energized Fasting and Qigong Retreat Sessions in the Bay Area include: hypertension, diabetes, insomnia, migraine, arthritis, vertebra ailments, skin diseases, kidney stone, intestinal and gastronomical problems, etc. Some famous TCM doctors and Qigong practitioners are among its beneficiaries. Their energy levels and healing skills were greatly enhanced.

Q-WHS is dedicated to benefiting more and more people from all over the world with its unique human training techniques. I hope that people will not view Q-WHS as just one opinion or one version of Qigong, but actually as one basis for the well-being of generations to come.

Zhang Yuan Ming

Sex: Male

Age: Thirty-three

Home: Cheng Du, China, and Tehachapi, California, U.S.A.

Began Studying Qigong: Age three

The Tradition of Qigong

I was born at Mt. Qing Cheng in Sichuan Province near the highlands of Tibet on the southwest border of China; a place known in ancient times as "Heaven on Earth." In this very special crossroads, a melding of culture took place among the Tibetan, Indian and Chinese traditions. The best of these traditions were nurtured, refined and passed along from generation to generation in my family lineage. For seventeen generations, my ancestors all followed special practices, acquiring wisdom through the study of longevity, health and the mystery of our Universe. Most prominent among them was Zhang Shan Feng, the founder of Taoist Taiji. Later, during the Ching Dynasty, several of my ancestors served as close advisors to the emperor, imparting their wisdom to their sovereign in the course of their governing duties. Through this heritage, I was destined to have a strong connection to traditional energy work.

My family promoted my connection to this heritage. As a little boy at the age of three, I began to meditate with my family. At the tender age of five, my grandfather brought me to meditate in the natural caves in the mountains, which had been inhabited by the China tiger and panda bear. As I got older, my father took me there to follow ritual fasting, drinking only fresh, spring water to sustain us. Every day, my grandfather taught me calligraphy. Every evening, my mother taught me, along with my four older brothers and sisters, breathing exercises and meditation until midnight. Sitting with legs crossed, we helped her sewing buttons and hems in collective, concentrated meditation. My special gift began to emerge as images spontaneously appeared in my mind while sewing. I enjoyed them immensely. In fact, during these meditations I had precognitive experiences encountering twenty of the twenty-four masters with whom I eventually studied in future years.

For thirty years now, I have been practicing and studying Qigong intensively. All my experiences have directed me down this path. Throughout my childhood, I studied with twenty-four different masters and hermits who passed down their special wisdom and teachings to me. Among them were experts in Chinese medicine, martial arts, Taoism and Tibetan Buddhism. At the age of twelve, I began to travel with my teachers, helping them treat people. At twenty, I was hired by the army to train their special forces in martial arts and Qigong. By 1988, all of my time and energy was devoted to the research and teaching of Qigong. In 1991, the United Nations Qigong Society invited me to teach and lecture on Qigong and I began to teach Qigong and martial arts throughout the United States.

Consistently, I have seen evidence of the power of Qigong to heal and benefit humanity and have become more aware of the importance of the special gift of my inheritance and training. For example, in 1988, as I was lecturing in Chengdu, among the audience of one thousand people, there was a man whose six-year-old nephew was hospitalized with leukemia. Listening to my lecture, this man began to think of the very sick boy who was in a remote area. It appears that his thought process set up a telepathic energy link for the transmission of Qi and simultaneously the boy was miraculously cured. This is just one example among many of the kind of occurrences in the field of Qigong healing that may seem fantastic but invariably take place. However, most healing arises when the individual, with time and patience, learns and practices Qigong for self-healing.

Although Qigong originated in China, it belongs to the whole world. My personal passion is to bring Qigong to the modern Western world so that, through study and practice, technologically oriented people can enter into the heart of a five-thousand-year-old cultural heritage. I travel extensively presenting experiential workshops to provide participants a firsthand understanding of the power of Qigong. Also, I have developed a series of videotapes in which I systematically present what I learned from my Masters in a suitable format for the people of today's world. Many people have told me that the methods presented in the workshops and tapes have helped them recover from health problems or allowed them to perform better at work. Qigong provides a vehicle to help us and our children cope with the sense of separation from nature and alienation from spirit. In my opinion, Qigong can provide the energy to help us fulfill our potential and even go beyond the limitations of our genetics. As our children understand the philosophy of Qigong and apply its principles, we can change our environment for the better and improve society as a whole. The best way that I can show appreciation for the incalculable treasure that I have received is to share Qigong with the people of the world in a manner that remains true to the traditions of generations, congruent with the needs of today, and strong and sustainable for the twenty-first century and beyond.

Zhao Zheng Rong

Sex: Female
Age: Twenty-three
Home: Beijing, China
Began Studying Qigong: Age ten

My name is Zhao Zheng Rong. I am a twenty-four-year-old Chinese woman [*in Western calculation, she's twenty-three; the Chinese believe we are one year old when we take our first breath—G.G.*]. I am very grateful that I have been given three wonderful gifts in my short lifetime.

The first gift was to be born in China this lifetime. I was raised in the homeland of Confucius. My parents were not wealthy with money, but were rich with the great traditions of Confucianism and Taoism and the ancient culture of our ancestors. As you might know, my homeland's traditions and practices are over five thousand years old. And with my parents' love and teaching, I gained a great knowledge and respect for these ancient traditions. From these traditions, I learned that for all human beings to have the greatest quality of life, to have the greatest ability to serve their family and their country, they must follow the Tao. My parents taught me that practices of Traditional Chinese Medicine and Chinese Kung Fu were very powerful ways to train the body and the mind to follow the Tao.

The second gift was the great love and wisdom of my mother and my father to allow me to follow an untraditional path for a young Chinese woman. I was not like the average Chinese daughter. I should have been quiet, but I was always talking and laughing. I should have studied the crafts of the woman, but I had so much energy that I wanted to run, to climb, to move, to explore. Within my family, this created a lot of confusion and tension. The nickname for me was "Crazy Girl." But my parents understood that I had to follow the Tao in my own way. My father was very wise. As he watched me grow, he realized that I could not thrive in a traditional school. And he set the direction for my life's work by allowing me to enter the Shaolin temple. As you may know, in China our policy is to have only one child per family. My country and my people make this sacrifice freely to help maintain the health of the world and the people. For my parents to allow their only child to enter the Shaolin temple at age eleven was a tremendous sacrifice. There I studied and practiced the art of Kung Fu. I was fortunate to enter the temple when the daily life was still very simple. I learned to train my mind, my body and my soul to gather and preserve the Qi. I can never express in words my gratitude for their wisdom.

The third gift was that the Tao led me to be a student of Master Wan Su Jian and a member of the Qigong Institute's family. The year of nineteen hundred and ninety (1990), Qigong was being reborn as an important way for strong health and a good life. My country helped

promote Qigong for the health of our people by provid-
ing classes in each province on Qigong. My mother was
working as a physician, trained in the Western medical
tradition, when she began researching Qigong with my
father. She had some recurring illness that did not
respond to Western medical practices. And my father
began to teach me the theory and practice of Qigong and
its relationship to Kung Fu. While reading a library book
on Qigong, I learned about the Qigong work of Master
Wan Su Jian. His life story and his work touched me so
deeply that I began to cry. And when I looked at his
photograph, I knew that the Tao was leading me to my
teacher. I felt a great respect for his courage to face hard-
ships and humiliations in order to bring Qigong theory
and treatment to the people of China. I knew from deep
inside my soul that I had to train and work with Master
Wan Su Jian. Like my father made it possible for me to
enter the Shaolin temple, he arranged with Master Wan
Su Jian for me to become a member of the Qigong
Institute. Over these nine years, I have had many rich and
varied opportunities to learn and to serve. As director of
Qigong theory and practice, I have the honor of recruit-
ing young students to enter the Kung Fu schools, then
advancing on the Qigong training at our Institute. And I
have continuing opportunities to teach and train and heal
visitors to our institute. As I experienced the pain that
poor health and empty minds cause, I am more committed to applying the teaching of the Taoist Masters. For the
Taoist Master, with few possessions and a very

simple life, always has a rich warm heart for the people.

Here are the thoughts that keep me close to all that I love each day. Hope you enjoy them. When I see the sun, I feel a great love from it. It reminds me of the teachings and love from my father and my great teacher. I think the sun just teaches us how to love people without any words. How great it is. When it is cloudy, the sun is hiding behind the clouds; this should be the best time for each of us to remember the wisdom within our own body. When I see the moon, it reminds me that the gentle energy is the best medicine to treat our hearts. She is just like our mother. She watches all of the children, all over the world. Can you hear her gentle voice: "My dear child, do not forget your mama is always here to watch you and love you." When I see the stars, I know these are the best gift from God, like a lot of diamonds hanging in the sky. They open and close their eyes to shine bright for us. Their lovely smile always reminds us: "Don't forget, return to yourself. We are all part of the Universe. We are all rich if we share our love with another."

Life is long. The Tao is part of the breath every day. Always remind ourselves, there is a very beautiful lotus flower in our heart. Just be at peace. Just breathe. You will rediscover your soul. We are all the same. And I believe one day, all of the people will know that we are one family on Earth, as part of the Universe.

I am honored to have an opportunity to express my heartfelt thoughts about the importance of Qigong for the health and peace of all nations. I know to follow the Tao will lead all of us to the richest life experience any person could hope for. I continue always as a student of Master Wan Su Jian and a Taoist. I hope in this way to work for world health and peace all of my life. I hope one day we can meet at our Institute in Beijing.

Eight
Qigong Visions

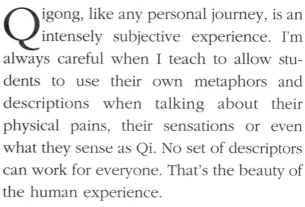

Qigong, like any personal journey, is an intensely subjective experience. I'm always careful when I teach to allow students to use their own metaphors and descriptions when talking about their physical pains, their sensations or even what they sense as Qi. No set of descriptors can work for everyone. That's the beauty of the human experience.

That said, it still proves to be valuable when we hear someone describe his or her unique sensations. Though it may be totally alien to us, the attempt to bring it into a common language is comforting. It gives us security that our own interpretation is just as legitimate. This is what we do for each other in this life. We help keep one another from feeling alone. Our attempt to put handles on what we feel allows others to be included in our Universe. As the sense of isolation is the curse of the ego, reaching out and sharing even the most outlandish feelings and thoughts in an atmosphere of acceptance is one of the more healing experiences in life. Allowing another person this freedom is an important component of love.

Qigong is one of those modalities that pushes us out of our "normal" existence and therefore stretches our lexicon. It requires a new "language" to describe sensations that we feel during its practice. Fine-tuning our sensitivity field to get in touch with Qi, to isolate the specifics of an ache or pain, or to sense the inner workings of another person, is the challenge of Qigong practice. These steps in our unfolding are unique to each individual. Though the words we use will be our own and reflect all of who we are, the essence will be the same.

In this chapter, I asked the following people to share their personal experience with this powerful healing modality. The question presented was: *What brought you to learn about Qigong, how would you define it, and how has it affected your life?*

Each of them comes from various walks of life. Some have practiced Qigong for years; for others, it's a relatively new experience. Some are expert practitioner/ healers and others are in pursuit of their own health.

It is an honor to me that each person revealed from his or her heart and shared with the hope of inspiring others. I trust that their perspectives will help you gain your own voice in understanding Qi and the essence of the Qigong experience.

Kenneth M. Sancier, Ph.D.

Sex: Male
Age: Seventy-eight
Occupation: Researcher and President, Qigong Institute
Home: Menlo Park, California, U.S.A.
First heard of Qigong: 1988

What Brought Me to Qigong?

Just after retiring from my career job as a senior chemist at S.R.I. International, where I usually worked on two to three major projects at any given time, I found myself without an intellectually stimulating substitute. The many interests I had in the arts, reading and people did not quite fill the vacancy.

Then about a year later, I discovered Chinese medicine and Qigong when I watched my regular television program on Saturday afternoons: *Asians Now.* That day, Dr. Effie Chow discussed Chinese medicine and her energy system and used an arm muscle test to demonstrate how body energy could be altered by Qigong. Such concepts had never been discussed in my scientific training. In fact, there are no words to describe "life energy" in English, much in contrast to the many words in other languages and cultures: Qi, Ki, prana, etc. So, I was amazed that body energy, or muscle energy, could be so easily and rapidly manipulated. The possibilities prompted me to enroll in Dr. Chow's seminar and later to conduct research with her on the subject, which has been published.[1] Another opportunity to study Qigong experimentally occurred in 1989 when I attended a conference in Hawaii on bioelectric energy. Among the participants at the conference were Qigong Masters and exhibitors who had specialized instruments for measuring the energy state of the body. I put members of these two groups together to study the effect of Qigong practice. The results showed that ten to fifteen minutes of Qigong practice balanced the energy system of the body.[2] I have continued my experimental research on Qigong, organized the Qigong Institute to improve health care through education and research, and became professor of research at the American College of Traditional Chinese Medicine. I have also presented scientific papers at international conferences on Qigong in Beijing, Shanghai, Tokyo, Vancouver, and I participated in organizing the First International Congress on Qigong in San Francisco.

What Is Qigong?

When I was being treated by my acupuncturist for a chronic respiratory condition, I asked him what type of Qigong would be best for me. The highly respected acupuncturist gave a very provocative response: "Most Qigong practices are basically the same, it is just important to circulate the Qi."

So, I wondered, what is the common denominator of Qigong practice to cultivate and circulate the Qi? I believe that the process includes exercises in awareness, intention, breath, posture, movement, touch and sound. These exercises first relax all parts of the body by reducing stress and tension. Then the mind can induce circulation of Qi throughout the body, and especially to parts of the body that are tense, diseased or injured. As the Qi is circulated, so the blood will follow. A basic tenet of Qigong and Traditional Chinese Medicine states that the mind leads the Qi, and the blood follows the Qi. An increase in blood flow increases delivery of oxygen and nutrients to cells of the body and removal of metabolic waste products. These improvements permit many functions of the body to operate at higher efficiency, including the immune system which is the key to fighting disease.

While many forms of Qigong may provide the benefits outlined above, not all Qigong forms are suitable for everyone, nor for any one person all the time. There are "neutral" forms of Qigong that almost everyone can practice, but there are others that may have adverse effects. I suggest beginners find a good teacher who preferably has some medical training in Qigong theory and Traditional Chinese Medicine. Otherwise, there are several fine books. In any case, approach learning Qigong in a relaxed and natural way. Qigong should be practiced regularly, just like brushing your teeth. Qigong is a way of life.

How Has It Affected My Life?

As a scientist, I find that Qigong has provided a significant intellectual challenge that equals or perhaps surpasses my profession as a research chemist. Practicing Qigong calmed my mind and made me less susceptible to some health problems.

References:

[1] Sancier, K. and Chow, E. "Healing with Qigong and Quantitative Effects of Qigong." *Journal of American College of Traditional Chinese Medicine.* 7.3 (1989) 13–19.

[2] Sancier, K., "The Effect of Qigong on Therapeutic Balancing Measured by Electroacupuncture according to Voll (EAV): A Preliminary Study." *Acupuncture & Electro-Therapy Research Institute Journal.* (1995) 119–127.

Anna Alvarez

Sex: Female
Age: Forty-three
Occupation: Oriental Medical Doctor
Home: Tallahassee, Florida, U.S.A.
First heard of Qigong: 1977

Qi Gong has become for me like a prayer. Each morning as I reach for the sky, I acknowledge the wonder and sacredness of the heavenly energy which is showered upon me. I am giving thanks for the warm return of the sun, and for all the celestial influences. I breathe out and feel the energy of Mother Earth. I give thanks for her generous gifts to all her creatures. I give thanks for the life blood of the waters and the rich beauty of the earthly mantle. I breathe in again and as I reach for the sky and draw heavenly energy down into my self, I remember my connection to both Heaven and Earth, and my being at the center, a mix of the two. I honor and acknowledge my special place in the great scheme of things and my connection with all things.

If my prayer ended there it would be enough.

But there are so many avenues to explore with Qi Gong. There are the intricate movements and utterances of the six healing sounds, the flexibility and coordination of the eight silk brocades, the endless ways of generating Qi and moving it through the micro and macro orbits. I can continue learning from one and all of these as well as literally thousands of Qi Gong forms to choose from.

It is my time to focus and be quiet, to go inside and yet stay connected to everything around me, and to the cosmos. I am made stronger by it in body, mind and spirit. It brings me back. It centers me. It strengthens me.

Qi Gong is also the foundation for the practice of Tai Ji. It warms my body and gets the blood moving. It works out the kinks in my skeletal and muscular systems. It makes me aware of the pull between Heaven and Earth as is reflected in my spinal alignment. It reminds me to let go of unnecessary tension anywhere. It grows my taproot into the Earth through my *Yong Quan* points in the soles of my feet so that I will be connected well to the Earth while I do my Tai Ji practice.

All day I can utilize Qi Gong. Even when I am standing in line at the grocery or the gas pump I can be aware of my connection. With any movement, there is potential to stay aware, connected. Putting away dishes, doing laundry, treating clients, greeting friends, moving in and out of buildings . . . it is a constant dance which doesn't end with the morning practice. The more I flow, the more life seems to easily flow around me and through me.

Life becomes a prayer.

Richard H. Lee

Sex: Male
Age: Forty-five
Occupation: Director of China Healthways Institute,
father of little Tomu who isn't so little any more.
Home: San Clemente, California, U.S.A.
First heard of Qigong: 1984

I was a consulting engineer, minding my own business, when I was introduced to a machine said to simulate the emitted Qi. Engineers can't resist the magnetic draw of a gadget (like perpetual motion machines) claimed to do something which seems impossible. Years of study seeking scientific understanding of that magic box were, at first fulfilling, but then, I started feeling that I was looking at Qigong from the outside.

I started taking courses on Qigong with excellent teachers, but I still felt like I was on the outside. Gradually I realized that it was because I hadn't devoted myself to practicing Qigong. After a few years of intensive practice, my view of the world has started changing. While I used to view science as the window into reality, I now see science as a window through which we can observe life. However, through Qigong practice I can move directly into life. It now appears that my scientific perspective separated me from life.

Up until two years ago, I would have defined Qigong

as the study of Qi, and then gone on to define Qi in terms of physics and psychology. I must say that this has changed. Qigong is "life exercise," practices or exercises which expand our consciousness, our awareness of being alive. Not just becoming healthy, but becoming aware of what health feels like. Not just expressing emotions, but experiencing (or mastering) the process of expressing (or not expressing) emotion. And not just thinking and understanding things about the world, but limiting the endless stream of thoughts and focusing the mind to become a channel for higher ideals and dreams.

Qigong awakens us to the realization that we are not our bodies, but rather, the spark of consciousness which resides within. Our health, emotions and thoughts are expressions of our body just as a blinking left-turn signal is an expression of our cars. As I discover more, I see how far I have yet to go. To me, a Qigong Master is one for whom all sense of personal self has vanished. The physical, emotional and mental activities of the body have chosen to serve that spark of consciousness within. Toward this end, I must practice discipline, calmness and focus, not just during Qigong exercises, but during all aspects of my life.

Janet MacPherson, M.R.E.

Sex: Female
Age: Forty-five
Occupation: Minister
Home: Toronto, Ontario, Canada
First heard of Qigong: 1993

Western medicine was all I needed. I considered myself healthy for my age and was very skeptical about any form of complementary medicine until my physician friend took to me hear Dr. Effie Chow's introduction to Chow Qigong. I had never heard of an energy system or meridians and my interest was sparked enough to want to learn more (mostly out of curiosity). So, I started four months of intensive training expecting nothing for my own health. I had accepted that the conditions I had were lifelong or a normal part of aging. Then the changes started happening.

During those four months, my migraines stopped and my doctor took me off the preventive medication that still had left me with migraines at least five days a week and three or four days a month off work, totally unable to function. I no longer needed the injections of Sumatriptan or the trips to the hospital emergency room for painkillers. The headaches have been gone for four years now, and it's been like getting my life back. If nothing else had improved, that would have been enough to convince me to practice Qigong and to want to teach others.

Regular bouts of respiratory distress had me carrying two inhalers and still I ended up in the emergency room with severe breathing difficulty. That stopped, and after a year of non-use I no longer carried the inhalers. The medication for a hiatal hernia was no longer needed. The early arthritis in my knees and hands was gone. I dropped twenty-five pounds and my sleep apnea improved. Through all of this, I had the guidance of Dr. Effie Chow and the benefit of individual sessions with her. Without her teaching and powerful Qi, I would not have known that healing was possible. In my first year of practicing Qigong, I saved thousands of dollars in drug costs.

Qigong is a way of life. It is much more than an exercise system; it is a discipline that can be learned by anybody. In the past four years I have seen the benefits that have touched all aspects of people's lives—the body, mind and spirit. Athletes; people suffering from serious, even life-threatening, illnesses; people in wheelchairs; the elderly; stressed-out business people have found that it improves their energy, productivity and quality of life. The physical exercises are gentle but very powerful. Rebalancing the Qi has eliminated troubling physical conditions and brought changes in mental attitudes.

The health system focuses on curing, rather than caring and healing. There can be curing without healing and healing without curing. Healing is much more than eliminating symptoms—it is attaining wholeness in whatever situation we find ourselves. Healing restores meaning in life. Practicing Qigong helps people take responsibility for their own well-being and manage their own health. The energy transferred by the healer is not controlled by him or her. It is a natural transfer of power.

Qigong enhances awareness of our connection to nature, to one another and to the source of all life. It is to embrace life with love.

Lee W. J. Chong Jie

Sex: Male
Age: Seventeen
Occupation: Student
Home: Singapore
First heard of Qigong: 1988

Since the time when I was young, I did not always have a very good impression of Qigong. That is because many so-called Qigong Masters in Singapore make use of Qigong to make money. Some of them open such classes, charging every student fifty dollars for four lessons per month, or using Qigong to cure illness. I am not saying that Qigong cannot be used to cure illness, but many of them are liars. They actually know nothing or very little about Qigong. The first time that I really came across Qigong was at the Third Singapore Taoist Day held in Singapore and organized by the Taoist Mission (Singapore). My Master from China, Master Huang Xin Yang brought with him six Qigong experts to perform. They did the Qigong on me and I really felt that Qi going through my body, then I believed in Qigong.

As to how Qigong has affected my life, it actually changes my lifestyle a little, as long as I practice it often. I even went on a month-long trip to Beijing, China, to specially learn Qigong from a well-respected Master there. Being a student and musician, I like practicing Qigong to clear my mind and to help me feel creative.

Daisy Lee

Sex: Female
Age: Thirty-five
Occupation: Filmmaker and television producer
Home: Toronto, Ontario, Canada
First heard of Qigong: 1995

My first conscious experience with Qi was on my parents' flower farm where I grew up in Newmarket, Ontario. Our neighbor, fifty-five-year-old Peter Wenzel, was having a well dug on his property and came running over to our farm, flushed with excitement. "Ve found vater!" he yelled in his thick German accent. "Fifty gallons a minoot!" Mr. Wenzel proceeded to shove a Y-shaped branch into my father's work-worn hands. "Hold," he said. "If stick pulls down, stop—zat iss vere vater iss." It sounded simple enough. My mother, father and then five siblings took a turn at the stick, but it didn't twirl or dance as Mr. Wenzel said he'd seen it do in the hands of his native friend.

By the time the branch came to me, my hands were sweating. Maybe that explained the reaction in them—the long end of the Y suddenly pulled towards the ground as if possessed by some strange magnetic force. I held the branch tighter, not trusting that I hadn't somehow willed the powerful surge of energy into my hands, but as I continued to walk, the branch started spinning in circles, faster and faster, until finally it snapped and cracked in two like a broken wishbone, startling everyone into silence. "Zere you go—you have a vater vitch in ze family," declared Mr. Wenzel.

Two days later, the well drillers informed us that we hit a gusher at close to one hundred gallons a minute. It was enough to support our family of eight, as well as twelve greenhouses that needed daily watering. We no longer needed to buy truckloads of water to be dumped into the cement cistern. My parents were ecstatic; finding water for a farmer was like striking oil for a Texan. At that time, I didn't know that what I felt in my hands was the vital life force or Qi that pulsed within the very Earth.

My second and, I hesitate to say, more official, encounter with Qi happened when my husband Eka was diagnosed with leukemia. A number of Qigong Masters heard about our search for a matching bone marrow donor, and had graciously offered their services to us free of charge. We didn't know what Qigong was, but heard it combined Tai Chi-like movements with energy and breath work, as well as some massage techniques. If done properly, Qigong could have extremely beneficial results for even chronic illnesses. One of the Masters, Dr. Hui, came to the hospital and showed me a few moves to break up the excruciating pain in Eka's abdomen without ever touching him. He asked me if I felt something between my palms as we practiced on Eka. Moments later, I recognized the same pulsing, magnetic force I felt as a child searching for water with a stick. It was like reconnecting with an old friend.

For several months, I worked on Eka using various Qigong techniques. It was very effective in treating acute pain and brought him much peace during stressful situations. It also helped eliminate morphine and codeine from his daily drug cocktail, but, in the end, it did not save this beautiful man's life.

I continued to study Qigong after Eka died and began using it on friends suffering from chronic illnesses like Lou Gehrig's disease and liver cancer, to acute pain sufferers of headaches and stomach cramps. After treating them for even a few minutes, they reported that the pain would start to dissipate; after about fifteen to twenty minutes, it was virtually gone. They woke up the next day feeling more refreshed and alert, and they slept peacefully throughout the night. I saw their faces light up with hope and enthusiasm as I started teaching them simple breathing techniques, visualizations and gentle movements. Their families often reported improvements in energy level and appetite, and eventually tried Qigong on themselves, having seen how helpful it was to their loved ones. Since these positive experiments, I've been encouraged to share what I know of Qigong and its many incredible healing capabilities.

When I practice Qigong now, I sometimes think back to that first encounter with Qi on the farm. It reminds me that this vital life force is everywhere around us, not just in the palms of our hands, or "two inches in and one inch below our navel at the Dan Tian." It is in the water, under the ground, in the air we breathe, the food we consume, and the people we interact with each day. In fact, all living things possess Qi, and as human beings, we have the opportunity to use it consciously to heal others and ourselves. Sometimes miracles happen and life is prolonged, and sometimes, we realize that life itself, whatever the length of time, is a miracle.

Kathleen Graf

Sex: Female
Age: Fifty
Occupation: Designer/Healer
Home: Lake Tahoe, California, U.S.A.
First heard of Qigong: 1985

Many long years ago (early 1970s), I found myself experiencing a near-death episode while being operated on. It was at that time I made a decision to come back. So for twenty-some years, I have been asking what my soul's purpose was through meditation and prayer. During this time I had studies with Dr. William Brugh Joy and started to delve into the deeper aspects of myself. Some not so easy to look at, but worth the pain. I have lived with three injunctions since then: no judgments, no comparisons and delete the need to understand. Continuing my search for answers, I studied with Dr. Carolyn Conger and Rev. Rosalyn L. Bruyere. There have been many other teachers along the way.

In the early 1980s, I studied Tai Chi from a wonderful Chinese woman in Aptos, California who said I must have done it in my past life, for it seemed second nature. Later, I studied it through the college here. I was introduced to Louis Sanchez and started taking his classes. It was in his Tai Chi class that he introduced us to Qi Gong.

In the summer of 1996, I found myself in Beijing,

China, attending the Third World Conference of Medical
Qi Gong. I thought I went there to see a healer named
Master Liu and to find out if there was anything I could
do to help friends and myself with back problems. A
force so strong was directing me. For over twenty years,
I have meditated and asked "What is my soul's purpose?"
"Why am I here?" "What is my life's work?" The answer
was presenting itself while I was in China. Being blessed
and able to stay there and be trained in medical Qi Gong
has changed my life.

So what is this thing called Qi Gong? It is a form of
exercise that is about five thousand years old and encompasses breathing, body movement and mind concentration. Through its practice it helps to open the meridians
and allows the Qi (life force) to flow in the body to heal
itself. What is so nice about Qi Gong is anyone can do
the exercises regardless of age or infirmity. Qi Gong has
given me the impetus to go back to school, after a long
career as an interior designer, and become a licensed
acupuncturist and hopefully a doctor of Oriental medicine—or whatever it takes to be the best medical Qi
Gong practitioner I can be. Thank you, thank you, thank
you.

Dr. Dennis Wilcox

Sex: Male
Age: Fifty
Occupation: Veterinarian
Home: Seattle, Washington, U.S.A.
First heard of Qigong: 1995

Qigong is a part of the ancient Chinese medicine phi-losophy. The Chinese believe that a deficiency or an excess of Qi (energy or life force) is the cause of disease. The study of Qigong teaches how to cultivate or build Qi, how to move it around the body for better balance and how to remove the excess. This is done with exercise, concentration and breath control. The Chinese believe that by doing these exercises, you can prevent or lessen the effects of disease, improve your health and increase longevity. Simply put, it works.

The study of Qigong has brought great rewards into my life. I have learned how to build my energy up when fatigued. When the pressures of daily living get out of control, I have learned how to quiet the mind, to filter out the irrational and unnecessary and only focus on the essential or nothing at all until calm returns. I have learned and am still learning to restrain my Western habits of forcing the outcome of events to my desire and to instead let them unfold for the highest good. This is a most difficult lesson but, when done well, the joy and beauty that is produced is beyond measure. Although in the past few years my life has taken several unexpected and unplanned changes—some would say catastrophic—the study of Qigong has been a major factor in my emerging from these trials as a confident, optimistic and joyous soul.

Audrey J. Schulenburg Brennan

Sex: Female
Age: Fifty
Occupation: Qigong Machine Guide, China Healthways
Institute
Home: San Clemente, California, U.S.A.
First heard of Qigong: 1992

Qi and Qigong were first introduced to me in 1992 when I began a new job marketing a health device based on it. Qigong Masters emit healing sound (and other energies) from their hands. This measurable low-frequency sound occurs naturally in all of us, although it measures very much stronger in Qigong Masters or practitioners who have the ability to use it to help relieve the pain and suffering of others. This instrument reproduces the same infrasonic alpha of the Masters. I did not experience emitted Qi energies for myself until four years later, on a company trip to China for a world conference on medical Qigong. In my mind, I am still there.

I never knew it was Qi when I was surrounded by it and already connected to it as a child growing up among the farmlands and riverfront fields back home. Nature, birds, wildlife, fresh air, aromas, cleansing thunderstorms, the four seasons, an ever-changing cycling and recycling of life, with thousands of stars in the sky each night whose energies tingled my skin. Much like that of

emitted Qi. Or the sensation arising in the personal practice of Qigong exercise and meditation. Now I see and
feel Qi everywhere. But it is not something easily
explained. You have to experience it for yourself.

Being in the presence of a Qigong Master, one is aware
of a soothing humbleness as powerful as his or her healing. It is my belief that the true Master's use of this healing energy is done with unquestionable good intention,
from the heart. At least this is the case with the Master I
choose to study with or be treated by. One thing I especially want others to know is that they too can develop
these healing energies, and through their own good
intention and practice, can take part in helping others.
And that helping others is what it is all about.

Becoming involved with Qigong has positively
changed me. I actually have a guilt complex about not
spending more time in its practice. I imagine the closer
you get to knowing Qigong, the closer you get to seeing
the order of the Universe, the living oneness we really all
are. The effect Qigong has on me and my life continues
and is never-ending.

Andreas Kuehne

Sex: Male
Age: Twenty-nine
Occupation: Kung Fu/Qigong Instructor
Home: Neustrelitz, Germany
First heard of Qigong: 1982

As a child, I loved reading science fiction books, mystical tales and strange stories. I read so much that in our small library in Neustrelitz, East Germany, I went through all those books I was interested in, available in the children/youth area, at the age of twelve. Being such a good customer, I was then allowed to go into the adult's area at that age. So in that way I became more and more interested in the wisdom of the ancient times from India, China, Japan, the Celts, the Egyptians, the Greeks and from others. I think that was the beginning. There appeared different names for the Qi concept and different ways. Then I met my first teacher, Kaikham Thammavong from Laos, along with some of his people.

Of course I will not define the word "Qigong"—that was done a lot. And when I start a new class and begin to talk about Qigong, I tell the students also the usual definition and talk about the Chinese Qigong. But later, I also tell other ideas. For me, I use the Chinese word Qigong, not because I think that I have to—for some kind of style or system thinking—but because I like the simple "energywork" (can be everything) and because I think that the Chinese brought something through the ages (maybe like the Indian people). It has developed but kept its basic simple idea living (for that I honor the Chinese tradition). In most other cultures, the same idea is forgotten a long time. Words alone are not important, styles and systems are not important, important is only the creative mind. So for me Qigong is not Chinese—the word is, some system is—Qigong in its essence is not Asian—it is human. But you have to use words in some moments, so I use "Qigong."

Qigong for me is the free mind, the creative mind. The mind, free and unlimited, but aware of the need of limitation for being and for unlimited change of the being form. Because I think there is no true form, so every form can be true. There is nothing at all, so there can be everything. It depends on the creative mind. Qigong is the way to cultivate, to harmonize the momentary form of existence. The moving moment. But using the word "way," I do not mean a way ready to go. I mean the way that everybody has to create by going themselves. So don't follow the Master! Learn from the Master and try walking and you will find no reason to feel to be at the end, but you never will be in a hurry and you can love the moment. So for me Qigong is the way to let the forms move, to create, to change. Nothing to get from the outside—trust, and you will always find more.

I learned to move my mind and to let go of limits, but use limits, by not believing in them. I can understand my body as a moving manifestation of my mind. I feel free. I can deal with my fears. I try to create my way and not to leave traces. I am healthy and satisfied by having lots of ideas and interests.

Doxie Jackson

Sex: Female
Age: Sixty-nine
Occupation: Chiropractor
Home: Corpus Christi, Texas, U.S.A.
First heard of Qigong: 1985

I involved myself with Qigong when I witnessed a broken leg heal in five days that had not healed in the two
weeks prior. This was in a fourteen-year-old person. This
healing was displayed via X rays. I have found that Qi is
the basis of all activity, the vitality seen in an active and
productive individual, which is responsible for much of
the recovery from illness and injury, which is clearly lack-
ing in patients suffering from chronic syndromes.

Everybody has Qi. The quantity and quality of Qi can
be increased through a series of specific, kinetic movements. In medical research in the United States, Qigong
has been shown to kill Gram positive and Gram negative
bacilli by swelling the cells. It kills viruses by dilution,
which produces a weakness in the virus. And it also
increases immune responses in both animals and plants.
The practice of Qigong cultivates Qi, which brings the
brain into coherence in the eight- to fourteen-hertz range
(alpha state).

Qi is full of potential; it is matter on the verge of
becoming energy or energy on the point of materializing.

Qi is like a neutrino—known in physics as a neutral particle having zero rest mass and no spin. All manifestations of Qi depend on change; the primary source of Qi never changes. From it, creation arises, and to it, all creation returns. This coincides with Western theory that matter and energy are essentially the same thing and can neither be created nor destroyed. Both simply contain the potential to assume different forms.

Qi forms the interface between the physical body and the belief system of the individual. Qi must always be completely chaotic, without structure, so as to allow swift and correct communication. Pain is a call for help from the body to the mind. If the Qi is weak or structured, the mind may not hear the call or the body may not hear the answer.

Qi has increased my ability to function on all levels, and I love teaching it to others.

Patrick Lugo

Sex: Male
Age: Thirty
Occupation: Senior Designer, Columnist and Creator of
the "Tiger's Tale" Comic for *Kungfu-Qigong* and
World of Martial Arts Magazines
Home: Berkeley California, U.S.A.
First heard of Qigong: 1995

Qigong is for everybody. Quite literally, there has yet
to be any other "thing" that can be the most use to
so many varied forms of life. Qigong can be called a science; it can as easily be called an art or simply a way of
life, depending on who is asked. I would call it the mastering of one's breath and as there is no one thing we, as
humans, do more than breathe; it should become evident
why Qigong can be of use to you.

Every moment of every day in our life is determined by
our breath. The slow easy breath of relaxation or the
deep ins and outs of excitement are just the most obvious examples of how our breathing reflects our being at
any given moment. If you are angry, then surely your
breath will reflect it. If you are nervous, then at least once
in your life you can recall being told to "take a few deep
breaths." The reasoning is varied but essentially the same:
Our breath determines our experience.

Now Qi or Chi can be translated as breath, it can also

translate into life or spirit or even life force. Like the Kung in Kung Fu, Gong can be translated to mean mastery. So while Kung Fu, which is most often infused with Qigong, could mean great mastery or ultimate achievement, Qigong could be made to mean mastery of the Qi or mastery of breath—why not even mastery of life?

Personally I have studied Kung Fu and other martial arts intermittently for about a third of my life. At thirty years of age, it has become evident that I've been practicing Qigong for considerably longer. Granted, I was unaware of the term Qigong until I began my work as artist for *Kungfu-Qigong* magazine in 1995, yet the path to my own mastery of Chi/life had been set long before that. With martial art training and endeavors into meditations of all sorts, even a period of time as a habitual smoker, I developed a finer and finer appreciation of a full breath of fresh air. It's been years since I freed myself from the habit of smoking and instead gladly continue the habit of breathing.

There are tons of different Qigong exercises you can learn. Methods that have been handed from generation to generation are probably still only known by select members of a given family. Meanwhile in China and more and more across the globe, systematized methods of Qigong practice are being taught to people of all sorts. For some, a strict regimen of specific exercises done at a specific time, even facing a specific direction can add immeasurable qualities to their life and health. Others, like myself, may well come across a variety of exercises and techniques in a sort of patchwork manner, learning certain techniques to remedy certain ailments or states of mind/experience; this one exercise is good to stop a headache while that one is good if you're cold or feeling lazy. The value in either is that you have available to you an action that can, and usually does, address a factor in your life that needs to have something done about it.

With each new technique learned, a greater understanding of both my own body as well as the general principles behind the art/science of Qigong blooms. Each such blooming expands the range of actions I have available to me as I move through life and its experiences. Less and less often do I find myself at the whim of circumstances; instead I have some available action to take.

If angered or upset, I have the choice to lose my temper and experience life through those consequences or use that Qigong exercise I know will bring me back to centered calmness; it's worked every time. If I find myself outside and not dressed warmly for the weather, I can shiver and chatter and probably complain about the cold or use this Qigong exercise that will "raise" my Qi and warm my body as well as give me the energy to get in out of the cold that much sooner. The list goes on and is only hampered by my ability and willingness to recall them as needed. Each time I have, I've benefited not just from the results but also from the knowledge that I can and will do so again. Thus the mastery of my life/Qi continues.

In the time that I have lived in northern California, I

have learned to infuse more and more of all that I do with the Chi that I am still learning to cultivate. This is evident in the work I do which sees publication as well as those endeavors which are of a much more personal nature. It's been said that talking to your plants inspires them to grow, Qigong in their presence will have equally positive results. I am fortunate in having knowledge of such value flow into my life, like a deep breath of fresh air, and I am grateful for each opportunity life grants me to pass such valued teaching on, like a contented sigh of relief.

I have spent the past several years in the San Francisco-Berkeley area of California producing interactive art events and dance parties where I make available Qigong techniques for those who wish to maximize their experiences and/or desire further means of mastering their own lives/Qi.

Michiko Iwao

Sex: Female

Age: N/A

Occupation: Pharmacist and Director, ARTI: Association
of Relaxation Therapy, International

Home: Kyoto, Japan

First heard of Qigong: 1988

Spreading a Tiny Seed
for Holistic Medicine

On June 22, 1988, I attended a Qigong workshop in
Japan. As the result of an accident five years previ-
ously, I had chronic pain at the waist. This date then
became the second birthday of my life. There I met my
Qigong Master Wan Su Jian, with eight young teachers
from Beijing. That was the first time I saw Qigong healing directed from outside towards the patient. For example, a girl who could not stand because of neuropathy
in the backbone could move her legs by using Qigong
healing. I could not understand what was happening so
I told Master Wan that I was a pharmacist in a Western
medical hospital. I wondered if Qigong became popular
in Japan, would I lose my job. I had just observed some
kind of flow that he had passed into her body. If it was
real, I thought medicine and Qigong should be linked.
Could drugs be delivered more easily into the body and

absorbed into the cells after Qigong healing? I wondered to him. Master Wan replied that exploring that point of view could be my life work. He asked if I would search more deeply and start Qigong training with them.

I then became a foreign student of his, and after seven months the pain at my waist disappeared. In 1990, Master Wan gave me the first diploma as a Qigong teacher of Bagua Xun Dao Gong and invited me to become a fellow of his Qigong Institute. Then I opened a Medical Qigong class in Japan with the name Association of Relaxation Therapy, International, and so it is now called ARTI. There I teach a self-care system and the healing methods of Bagua Xun Dao Gong.

In 1993, Dr. S. Kajiyama, in the department of metabolic internal medicine at Kyoto City Hospital, called on me. One of his elderly patients announced to him that she could stop medication and keep her blood sugar level by using only diet and the Qigong walking in an ARTI class. Dr. Kajiyama then asked me to teach Qigong walking to other patients. I completed Qigong walking as a thirty-minute exercise program for diabetics. Dr. S. Kajiyama researched its medical effects. Mild and slow exercise is necessary for patients who are elderly with some complications. While vigorous exercise increases pulse rates and uses sugar rather than fat as a source of energy, Qigong walking does not cause a large increase in pulse rates and reduces blood sugar after a meal in diabetic patients. The measurements were also taken on a day with no exercise after lunch as a control. The data were analyzed by ANOVA [*a medical research organization in Japan—G.G.*] with repeated results. This case study indicated to me that Western medicine became more beneficial when combined with Qigong. Patients could control their disease independently by using Qigong walking. In 1997, I reported this at The World Diabetic Conference in Beijing and The Second World Congress on Qigong in San Francisco. As a pharmacist and Qigong teacher, the seed that I am trying to spread is very tiny now, but it could be a benefit as conventional wisdom for human beings in the twenty-first century.

A traditional saying in Daoist medical Qigong is that Qigong, Wuji [*spiritual practice—G.G.*] and medicine are as one. In the case of spending time only practicing Wuji without Qigong, you will spend your life as a child playing. In the case of spending your days only in practicing Qigong without Wuji, you will make your life difficult without realizing it. In the case of spending your time in studying both Qigong and Wuji without studying medicine, you will never find what your life exists for. I keep this saying in my life, and I will make a network for the spread of holistic medicine.

Barbara Bernie

Sex: Female
Age: Eighty
Occupation: Chairman/CEO American Foundation of
Traditional Chinese Medicine
Home: Hillsborough, California, U.S.A.
First heard of Qigong: 1980

I have just awakened. It is 6 A.M. I am in a quiet room, and I open the window to let some fresh air in. After a few stretches and deep breaths, I sit on the edge of a chair with my legs spread apart as far as my shoulders and at right angles to the floor. My body is straight, but relaxed, and all my weight has dropped to my hips. My eyes look straight ahead into the distance, and I close them. My tongue touches the roof of my mouth, and my mouth is closed. I breathe in and out of my nostrils and my mind is on the Dan Tian point, three fingers below the navel. My hands are resting lightly in my lap, one hand in the palm of the other. I am relaxed. All the thoughts on my mind of today's plans, problems to be solved, work to be completed—gone. At this moment, I dismiss everything. I return to the quiet of my breathing and focus on where it is going. Breathing into the abdomen, filling the cavity with Qi. After a while I begin to feel energy tingling in my fingertips, going down to my toes. My body and hands get warm. I sit this way for about twenty minutes. My mind is clear; I am calm. I feel energized and ready for the day's work.

I am practicing Qi Gong, which predates and is the root of Traditional Chinese Medicine (TCM). TCM is based on a system of energy that flows along pathways called meridians. When there is blockage in the meridian or an imbalance, the body breaks down and has pain or other problems. Qi Gong is a discipline, and if it is practiced properly and with dedication, you can become aware of blockages or imbalances in your system and be able to resolve them by practicing these meditative breathing exercises.

In 1980, I was diagnosed with ovarian cancer. I had surgery in California for the removal of a tumor, which had metastasized. I needed to be on chemotherapy. As a practitioner of TCM, I knew the value of combining TCM with chemotherapy. Unfortunately, at the time of my surgery it was not possible to arrange that in California or the United States. On previous trips to China, I had met many TCM practitioners and also an oncologist. After many conference calls to find out how they would treat my cancer, they told me that I would be treated with a combination of TCM and chemotherapy. And they invited me to have treatment in Shanghai. In 1980, I was certainly the first and perhaps still the only American who went to China to be treated for cancer. Along with the chemotherapy and TCM, I was also introduced to the practice of Qi Gong, which has become one of the most important practices of my life.

I define it as simple meditative breathing exercises that fill and expand the lungs and abdomen with air and oxygen, which activates and nourishes the whole circulatory and organ system. Qi is the essence that keeps everything in motion and functioning. It is life's force. Without it, nothing moves and there is death.

Most mornings I awaken at 6 A.M. and practice Qi Gong from twenty minutes to one hour. If I skip a couple of days without practice, I really feel it. My voice is not as clear, my energy, spirit and mental alertness are all affected. Therefore, I do try to discipline myself and do it every day. Today, I am planning programs for children so that they can benefit from this practice and be in charge of their health and well-being.

I am a woman, eighty years old, and first learned about the practice of TCM almost thirty years ago when I had what is known today as chronic fatigue syndrome. Because it helped me overcome my illness, I embarked on a lifetime journey of study and practice. In 1980, at the time that I had surgery for cancer, I was given at the most, five years to live. And now it is almost twenty years later. I have much to be thankful and grateful for TCM and especially for the practice of Qi Gong.

Nine
Wuji Qigong

Outwardly, Qigong is simply a physical exercise system that involves stretching and intentional breathing. Upon deeper study and dedicated practice, the transformative and holistic nature of this health maintenance modality becomes clearly apparent. Balancing the ancient traditions of China, Wuji Qigong has been passed down through Master Duan Zhi Liang. It seeks to strengthen the body (the mandate of the Taoists) while enhancing spiritual life (the essence of the Buddhist doctrines) and ultimately help the health of others (the basis of Christianity). Ultimately, a merging of the three takes place, not intellectually, but through *wu xing* or deep, emotional and spiritual understanding. At this point, we realize that Qigong is not tied to dogma but becomes a personal journey of discovery. After practicing Qigong, like any endeavor, it becomes second nature. It is then that the *form* of the movements we make becomes secondary to the inner transformation that emerges.

Written and oral teaching can only seek to trigger and stimulate you, the true wu xing must come from within— as the truth derives from Nature and is constantly accessible to you. Through cultivating your inner Qi, you become strong, not as an "individual" against the world but as an integral part of the world—a mirror reflecting light. This serves to awaken our compassion for others and ourselves. Sincere practice with an intention to gain balance and enhance sensitivity is the key to experiencing the full benefits of Qigong.

The following forms are examples taken from thousands of Qigong styles taught throughout China. I have selected them as they are easy to learn yet produce noticeable results with regular practice. I share the Wuji Hundun (chaos) style taught to me by Master Duan Zhi Liang because it resonates deeply and has proven to be effective for many people. The Bagua Xun Dao Gong Qigong warmers are ancient Taoist techniques incorporated into Master Wan Su Jian's health-care system. I learned the closing moves, that I present at the end of this chapter, at the Shaolin Temple. As both Master Duan and Wan studied there, it seems natural to close with these complementary techniques.

Taken together, I hope you will find them to be a very comprehensive health maintenance and healing routine. Do as much or as little as you are able. Please consult a physician before doing any physical exercises such as these, especially if you feel in any way that you may be straining yourself.

Master Duan constantly reminds me to "mix up" the eighteen Wuji Hundun forms. It's called "chaos" for a reason, as I described in the introduction. Let the system become your own. Put it together in a way that feels right for you. If there are just a few that work for you, stick with those and practice them regularly. You ultimately are responsible for making something "good" for you or making it "bad" for you. Listen deep. Your body will tell you.

Enjoy.

Basic Forms

Note: *These exercises are designed to gather heavenly Yang and earthly Yin forces. They will help to cultivate your Nei or inner Qi and build your lower Dan Tian, your body's center of gravity, located just below your navel. They will also teach you to build your Wei or external Qi, which is considered to be an important aspect of your body's immune system. Once you become comfortable with these exercises, try and work up to doing a minimum of three sets of each move. Maintain a relaxed posture throughout this workout, standing with your feet shoulder width apart, keeping your shoulders dropped and rounded, and your buttocks tucked slightly in as this will help keep your spine straight. Keep your breathing steady and deep, focusing on your diaphragm. Squeeze in to exhale, sucking your belly in, and expand your diaphragm, pushing your belly out, to inhale. Visualize Qi, or life energy, flowing to follow your hand movements and guided* *by your intention and mental focus. Most importantly, have fun and stay joyful as you practice and "play" Qigong.*

Warmers:

Morning Release

Palms facing together at lower Dan Tian (just below navel), spread hands about thirty-six inches apart while exhaling. Bring hands together to about one inch apart while inhaling . . . slow, steady diaphragmatic breathing. Do this three times. Bring hands straight up the midline, palms facing upward until you reach the middle Dan Tian or chest level, then rotate palms so they face heaven, fingertips touching, exhaling through the mouth and making an audible "Ahh" sound . . . building volume until your hands are extended overhead, arms are straight and elbows locked, and you've completely exhaled. While hands are straight overhead, face palms downward and bring them down the midline to the lower Dan Tian. Repeat three times.

Wuji Swimming Dragon

This beautifully simple warm-up exercise evokes a "swimming dragon" moving through the ocean. With knees bent and shoulders dropped and feet shoulder width apart as before, reach out to the side with your right hand, palm facing up to gather Yang energy from heaven. Continue the arc of this motion forward . . . keep your shoulder loose. When your hand is out in front of you and your arm is straight, slowly turn your palm to face the Earth, gathering Yin Qi, bending your elbow as your palm nearly touches your lower Dan Tian, just below your navel. Continue the motion of your right hand, barely brushing your body. Push your hand straight back behind you, continuing the smooth arcing motion out to the side. Repeating this complete motion with your right hand and begin the same movement with your left, starting when your right hand is extended off to the right. Continue this "swimming" motion for three to five minutes, breathing deep, coordinating inhalations with your right hand moving toward your body and exhalations with your right hand moving away from your body.

Bagua Xun Dao Gong
"Heaven, Man, Earth" (Tian Ren Di)

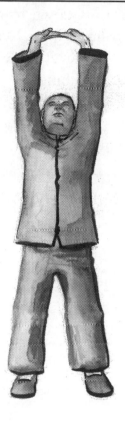

Part One: Palms face together at the level of the lower Dan Tian, knees slightly bent, feet shoulder width apart. Spread hands wide apart to the sides while inhaling . . . palms facing each other throughout, bring hands together to about ten inches apart in front of your lower Dan Tian while exhaling. Repeat three times. Palms facing upward, fingertips together, raise hands straight up while inhaling at the middle Dan Tian, chest level, rotate wrists so palms face away then upwards again until your arms are straight above your head and your elbows are locked with finger-tips touching. Bring arms down to either side, rotating your wrists so your palms remain facing toward Heaven, stretched out to shoulder level while exhaling . . . slow, steady diaphragmatic breathing . . . raise hands above your head, palms facing each other, to about twelve inches apart . . . open arms wide again back to shoulder level. Do this three times.

Part Two: With arms extended to each side at shoulder level, turn palms facing downward, while exhaling, bring palms down as if your arms were wings, bending wrists and elbows. Bend knees as far as comfortable, keeping your spine straight and knees directly over your toes. At your lowest point of squatting, turn palms upward, begin straightening your legs, bringing hands to shoulder height, returning to the starting position. Do this three times.

Part Three: With arms out to the sides, elbows locked, turn palms downward and bend at the waist, doubling over as far as you are able—making sure your neck is fully relaxed and your head goes down first. Keep palms facing the Earth, bringing the base of your palms together. While still bent over, open up your arms like wings and then bring the base of your palms back together. Do this three times. Finally, place palms as near as you can to the top of your feet. Lay your palms directly on the point between your big toe and first toe, one inch in from the web (key Liver point) if you are able. Inhaling with one deep breath, guide your Qi, with your hands touching your body, up the inside of your ankles, up the inside of your legs (moving along your spleen meridian) cross your hands across your lower Dan Tian, keeping hands gently touching your body. Move your hands up the sides of your ribcage, right hand on left side of abdomen, left hand on right side, (which passes your hands over key spleen and liver points), straighten up your body as your hands move up the midline to the upper Dan Tian—your head should be the last body part up as you extend both arms directly overhead. We will repeat this sequence once more.

Eighteen Forms of the Wuji Style

The concept behind the first and the last of these eighteen forms is that we begin in "birth" or sunrise and end with "death" or sunset. This death is actually a beginning, and could be thought of as a rebirth. The inner sixteen forms are designed to be practiced in random order, honoring the chaotic nature of the Universe. This helps stimulate the intuitive right-brain functions rather than the linear and ordered left-brain intellectual functions. Mix it up and make it your own.

Wuji is made up of two Chinese characters: The first is *wu* which means "nonbeingness, no-thingness," and second is *ji* which refers to "limit, end, ultimate." As you can see, this concept evokes many feelings. My ninety-two-year-old teacher in China, Master Duan Zhi Liang, is the lineage holder for this family-held system that's been around in this form for over twelve hundred years. One way he describes Wuji is that it is "the infinite moment of creation, that transition between formlessness and form, between dreams and reality." It is through your practice and meditation that you will come to experience Wuji for yourself. Enjoy the journey. . . .

Zhao

The beginning movement, the image of sunrise, of birth. With feet together, arms relaxed and hands at your sides, breathe deep with your diaphragm. Ease into your balanced posture. Relax your eyes to widen your vision while slightly lowering your eyelids. Make a gentle "scooping" gesture with your hands, bringing the "scoop" up to your lower Dan Tian, palms facing upward with fingertips touching . . . inhale, visualizing your Qi moving up from your feet to your middle Dan Tian as your hands move to your heart level. Turn your palms to face downward . . . exhaling, push your hands back down to your lower Dan Tian. With arms fully extended downwards, elbows locked and hands stretched to create a ninety-degree angle with your forearms and fingertips touching, rotate your hands outward so your fingertips are pointing behind you as far as you can twist your wrists. Raise your arms slowly to the sides while still extended . . . up over your head, palms now facing to the front. Stretch upward, opening your shoulder joints in the process, with arms still stretching upward, bring the Lao Gong points in your palms together as if in prayer. Continue stretching, getting up on your toes if you are able. Still in "prayer" bring your hands down, fingertips facing upward until your forearms are parallel with the ground. Separate your hands while extending your arms straight out in front of you, palms facing upward. With arms fully extended, turn palms to the Earth, open and stretch the shoulder joints. Slowly drop your arms to your sides. Bring your hands up to cross across your breast . . . right hand first against your chest, left arm over right . . . the middle finger of each hand presses into your Lung 1 point (Zhong fu), in the indentation just under your collarbone (clavicle) right next to your shoulder. Drop your head and rotate fully clockwise around once then counterclockwise. Lift your head back up, stretch your arms straight out in front again as before, palms down, then lower back to your sides. Put your weight on your left leg and step to the right. As you do this, your hands form the Wuji mudra (hand position), while you imagine you are holding a small ball of Qi, thumb touching pinky finger of each hand.

When finishing this move and each of the Wuji Qigong moves, return to the rest position—palms facing the belly at the lower Dan Tian, about six inches away . . . shoulders round and relaxed, knees slightly bent.

Note: *Your thumb is at one end of your Lung meridian and your pinky is at one end of your Heart meridian. When they touch, a circuit is created between the Heart system (representing joy) and the lung system (representing grief). It is believed that the joy of the Heart can ease the grief of the Lung and this hand position is a tonifying and balancing technique.*

Rou
Rolling ball of Qi

Palms facing together at lower Dan Tian, knees slightly bent, imagine you are holding a volleyball with hands on opposite sides. Move right hand to top, left to bottom of the "ball." Roll this imaginary ball for a minute or two, breathing deeply into it. Use your visualization skills to "see" and "feel" it. Keeping your back straight, turn your torso to the right, exhaling, left hand moving to the top of the "ball" as you reach your limit. Turn forward, inhaling, right hand moving to the top of the ball; then, when facing forward, both hands are at the sides of the ball. Turn to the left, exhaling, right hand moving to the top of the ball as you reach your limit. Turn slowly to face forward, inhaling, left hand moving to the top; then, when facing forward, both hands are at the sides of the ball. Move slowly and smoothly.

Note: *This exercise is designed to stretch the muscles and tendons around your spinal column and shoulders and can help prevent osteoporosis. Done correctly, it flexes your knees and ankles while opening the six Yin and Yang meridians of the arms.*

Chai
From center chest, press diagonally

Raise your imaginary ball of Qi from your lower Dan Tian to your middle Dan Tian, in front of your chest. Extend your right hand, fingertips facing up, to the right side and up at a forty-five-degree angle, bending into your right leg slightly. Turn your torso and look up at your right hand. Simultaneously extend your left arm, fingers also facing upward, down to the left. Your arms should make a straight line. Turn to face front as you "scoop" the space in front and below your lower Dan Tian with both hands, bringing the energy and Qi to that spot, then raising your Qi to your middle Dan Tian again. Repeat the move to your left side. "Scoop" again, but this time push your right hand straight up, elbow locked, palm facing Heaven and fingertips facing your midline. Simultaneously push your left hand straight down, elbow locked, palm facing Earth, and fingertips facing your midline. Bring your hands together at your middle Dan Tian as if you were compressing your ball of Qi, and reverse hand positions, right arm down and left arm up. Finish by compressing Qi at your middle Dan Tian, then move your intention, following your hands, to your lower Dan Tian.

Note: *This move is excellent for moving congested Qi from the lungs and opening the Yin meridians of the arms.*

Xuan

Palms to Earth, rotate side to side

Hold your hands at the level of your lower Dan Tian, palms facing the Earth and fingers gently outstretched as if they were lying on a flat surface. Inhale as you turn your torso around to the right. Turn as far around to face behind you as possible without twisting your neck. At this farthest point, your wrists should just touch your belly. Without stopping, begin exhaling and turning to the front while slowly pushing your hands, always parallel to the Earth and at lower Dan Tian level, away from you. They are farthest away when you are facing forward and have completed your exhale. Inhale as you begin turning to the left, slowly bringing your wrists close to your body as you did to the right. Return to the front, exhaling. Repeat each side two more times.

An
Pressing side to side and front to back

Guide your imaginary ball of Qi from your lower Dan Tian to the middle Dan Tian. Extend both arms outward, parallel with the ground, fingertips facing heaven. Keep your hands within your peripheral vision as you look straight ahead. Next, look over your right shoulder and gently turn your head to stretch your neck, looking as far back as possible. Turn back to look at your right thumb

. . . holding that focus, slowly pull your right thumb to your nose. Keep your elbow at shoulder height . . . hold your focus on the thumb. Continue to push your right hand to the left so that both arms are parallel. Stretch your shoulders . . . keep your spine vertical . . . pull your right hand back, using your shoulders to make the initial retraction. Hold focus on the right thumb until it nearly touches your nose, then release your focus and look straight ahead. Right arm continues moving to return to its fully extended position out to the right. Repeat this with the left arm. When left arm is complete, move both extended arms so that they are facing in front of you, parallel with the ground. Pull the right hand back, focusing on the thumb, until it nearly touches your nose. Continue the movement, turning your head and torso to stay focused on the right thumb. Extend your right hand behind you, keeping your left arm in its original position. Stretch the shoulders. Pull your right hand back so your thumb just touches your nose . . . turn to front . . . both arms parallel. Repeat with the left arm.

Note: *A large component of this move is an eye exercise which can prove quite beneficial. Focus on exhaling with all arm extensions and inhale with contractions. This move helps to open shoulder meridian pathways and stretch/cleanse Yin meridians in your arms.*

Si

Fingertips at Lung 1, rotate shoulders in circles

As a counter-stretch to the previous move An, bring the tips of all your fingers together and press them against acupressure point Lung 1 in the indentation below your collarbone and between your shoulder and pectoralis chest muscle of the same-hand side. Keep elbows facing toward Earth. Begin by inhaling and making a scooping motion with your right elbow, moving it upward, over your head. As you exhale, continue that circular motion, stretching your elbow behind you until it returns to the starting position. Repeat this with your left arm and again with your right several times.

Note: *This is an excellent exercise to heal sore shoulders or damaged rotator cuffs. The arm is not extended so there is less stress on the joint when rotating.*

Jian
Two fingers together like parallel swords

Extend your index and middle fingers while holding your ring and pinky fingers with your thumb. Point these fingers away from you and keep them parallel with the Earth at the level of the lower Dan Tian. Hands should be about nine inches from your body. As if the fingers of both hands were locked together in their parallel positions, move them up in an arch to the right to forehead level, elbows locked, inhaling. Fingertips always facing away from you. Swing them back down to their original position, exhaling. Inhaling, swing them up to the left side. Exhaling, return to their original position. Inhaling, move up to the right. Rotate your wrists so that your fingertips point to the right and are parallel to the Earth and each other. Move them in unison to your left side, keeping them at eye level. When you've moved them to the left and can no longer keep them parallel to each other, rotate your wrists so your fingertips face to the left. As before, move your hands as far as you can to the right side. Cross your hands in front of your middle Dan Tian and return to the rest position.

Note: *This is a good exercise for treating carpal and ulnar tunnel syndromes or strain from too much typing.*

Chan

Fingertips together, rotate, move down sides

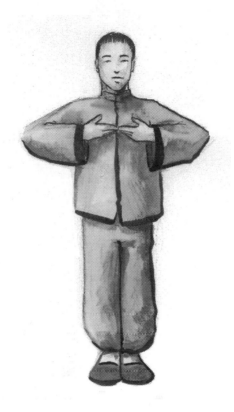

Move your hands in front of you, palms facing away . . . fingertips touching. Your arms form a gentle circle . . . parallel to the ground . . . push away, locking elbows . . . fully extended fingers at a ninety-degree angle to your forearms. Twist your hands outward, keeping your arms straight, twisting the wrists and forearms. Your fingertips now facing the Earth, bring your fingertips up, facing away from you, then toward you. Continue pushing them downwards then stretching away from you with arms fully extended. Pull your hands toward your body, keeping fingers extended and palms facing the earth. Elbows stay close to your sides . . . push both palms down until your elbows are locked. Release any tension in your shoulders. Repeat this move two or three times.

Note: *This is a classic move for improving digestion and relieving both diarrhea or constipation, since it balances the Qi in the lower abdominal area.*

Kun

One hand in front, fingertips up, other hand on back

Begin by moving your right hand, fingertips facing upward, to the level of your middle Dan Tian and about seven inches away from your chest. Twist wrist so palm is facing slightly away from you and your thumb is behind your index finger. Simultaneously, bring your left hand as close to your upper back as possible, with back of hand lying flat against your spine. Once settled in this position, slowly turn your torso as far as you can to the right, trying not to twist your neck and exhaling to the farthest point of the turn. Begin inhaling while turning to the front. Start exhaling as you turn all the way around to the left side. Once turned as far as you are able, begin exhaling slowly as you turn to face front. Whip your left arm around to the front, locking elbow and keeping palm facing Heaven. Stop when your left arm faces directly in front of you, parallel with the ground. Smoothly swap hand positions and repeat the same turn and breath com-binations to each side.

Note: *This is a good exercise for increasing shoulder flexibility and opening blockages in the heart and lungs.*

Coa

Arms to sides, pulling fingertips, then overhead

Extend your arms to each side, parallel to the Earth, palms facing forward, fingertips extended. Curl your right hand inward, fingertips leading, and "push" your hand across your chest. Continue this gentle pushing along the inside of your left arm. With your right hand, grab the fingers of your left hand and gently stretch them. Turn your head and look behind you as far as you are able without straining. Next, swap hands so that your left hand is stretching the fingers of your right hand. As you make this swap, turn your head to face forward. Complete this phase by "pulling" your right palm back across your left arm and extend it out to the right. Repeat this procedure with your left hand.

Liu
Great ball of Qi, rolling side to side

From the rest position, slowly expand your imaginary ball of Qi until your arms are fully extended and your elbows are locked. Keep your palms facing each other and try to feel their connection even at this distance. Roll this great ball, imagining that its center is your lower Dan Tian. Keep your shoulders and hips loose and flexible as you roll this ball around for a couple of minutes.

Rao

Base of palms together, rotate figure eight

Touch the heels of your palms together a few inches in front of your lower Dan Tian. With fingers relaxed and slightly extended, rotate your wrists in a figure-eight pattern. Keep your elbows and shoulders relaxed and supple. Over-accentuate this move to obtain the best stretch of your wrists and forearm muscles and tendons. Maintaining contact between your wrists, pull your hands toward your shoulders and then push away while continuing to rotate your wrists.

Note: *This is an excellent treatment for carpal and ulnar tunnel syndromes. It is also helpful for any sore or strained wrists, especially pain coming from stiffness due to extensive typing.*

Tuoa

Snake-like movements around your head and torso

This is the signature move of the Wuji style. Start with hands at the sides of your hips, palms facing Heaven. Push your right hand forward and to the left until your arm is fully extended. Continue the movement by moving your right hand far to the right. Continue this arcing movement until the back of your hand is directly over your head, above your Bai Hui point. Keep your palms facing Heaven throughout this entire move. Continue the circular movement of your right hand as you push it far to your right, focusing on keeping your shoulder loose. Continue the movement, pushing your right hand behind you and returning your hand to the starting position. Repeat this move with your left hand. Next, start with your right hand and when it is at the Bai Hui point, begin moving your left hand through the sequence. Continue moving both hands and maintain this relationship; one will be above the head while the other is at the waist.

Note: *This is an excellent exercise for loosening tight shoulders and rebuilding weak rotator cuffs. The traditional way to train in this move is to place a round stone in the palm of each hand and try not to drop it during the movements.*

Xia

Like Si only move elbows straight up and down

Place fingertips together and press them into the Lung 1 point next to your shoulders and below your collarbone, maintaining contact throughout. Push your right elbow up so that it points to Heaven and simultaneously push your left elbow down and slightly behind you. Swap positions and repeat a few times.

Moa
Rubbing lower Dan Tian and windmill actions

Both hands cover the lower Dan Tian. Women should have left hand on top of right, and men should have right on top of left. Press against your belly and make a circular motion: eight circles in one direction and eight in the opposite direction. Stick out the pinky finger of your right hand, holding the remaining fingers of that hand with your thumb. Move your right hand in an arcing motion

from your lower Dan Tian, up and outward until your
arm is extended out to the right. Continue moving your
arm down as you bend your torso down. Bend your left
leg as you do this, keeping your right leg straight.
Continue the circular movement of your right arm, swing-
ing it straight down and up to the left. As your arm
swings to the left, shift the weight of your legs, now
bending your right leg and keeping your left leg straight.
Allow your torso to bend to the left as far as you are able.
Bring your extended right arm up over your head, down

to your right side, and then return your hand to your lower Dan Tian. Repeat this complete move with your left arm. Next repeat this sequence with your right arm only this time extend your index and middle fingers, holding your ring and pinky fingers with your thumb. Repeat this move with your left arm. Follow this with your right arm again but extend your middle, ring and pinky fingers, holding your index finger with your thumb. This move is slightly different as you should reach back and to the right when your arm is moving in the downward stroke and then a bit forward and to the left as you are coming up. This cuts through your Qi field in a diagonal motion rather than the previous side-to-side action. Repeat this with your left hand. The final phase of this move requires you to form your right hand into a tiger's claw, bending your fingers as if you were to scratch something. Drop your hand to the side and back behind you as you arch your spine backwards. Be careful and only go back as far as you are comfortable. Allow your head to drop back fully and gently. Extend your right arm fully behind you and move it up over your head as you gently stand back up. Continue the arc of your right arm as your clawed hand returns to your lower Dan Tian. Repeat this with your left hand.

Note: *Though this is an excellent exercise for strengthening your lower back, opening the Spleen, Liver and Kidney channels in your legs, and energizing your spine in general. Please be cautious not to strain yourself. It is better to stretch and build up slowly to avoid hurting your back.*

Xun

One arm front, the other back, rocking wrists

Bring your hands together about a foot in front of your lower Dan Tian, palms facing. Imagine you are rolling a small, two-inch ball between your hands. Slowly alternate this action with imagining that there is a sponge between your palms, slowly compressing and expanding this imaginary sponge a millimeter at a time. Continue until you begin to feel a sensation between your hands. Be patient. Once you feel this, pull your right hand, palm facing your midline, past your torso and straight back behind you. Simultaneously push your left hand out in front of you. Both palms are facing the same direction, to your right. Twist your right palm so that it faces the opposite direction. Bending your knees and both your elbows, make a "chopping" action with both hands as they return to the starting position of this move. Repeat this sequence on your left side.

He
Palms overhead, then in front, rotating torso

Open your arms to each side, palms facing Heaven. Continue this action simultaneously with each arm until your palms are about eighteen inches above your Bai Hui point at the crown of your head. Shoulders should be relaxed and arms relaxed and in a round arc. Focalize heavenly Yang Qi into your body through the Bai Hui. Slowly exhale as you rotate your torso and turn to the right. Do not turn your head, keep it fixed, moving in relation to your upper body. Inhale as you turn to the front. Repeat this to the left side and return to the front. Exhaling, slowly drop your hands in front of you so that your arms are parallel with the Earth. Keep your arms in a curve so that they form a circle together, fingertips almost touching. Continue your exhalation as you turn your torso, as before, as far right as you are able. On your inhale, turn to the front. Exhaling, turn to the left. Inhale on your turn to the front. Slowly gather Qi as you return your hands to the rest position, palms facing your belly and about six inches away.

Hui

The Sunset: Arms scoop to Heaven, wrists together

Cross your wrists in front of your lower Dan Tian and as you inhale, raise your hands above your head with wrists still touching, palms facing toward you. Exhale and open your arms to the sides. Gather Qi toward your lower Dan Tian with palms facing your belly. Position your hands to hold a ball about nine inches in front of your lower Dan Tian so that each thumb touches the pinky on the opposite hand, palms facing each other. Take one step back in honor and humbleness.

Exhale deeply and relax.

Close
Shaolin Tui'na

This is a daily routine used as both a close to the Wuji Qigong set and a stand-alone morning treatment developed at the Shaolin Temple. Perform each of these self-healing techniques in sequence while standing in the "rest" position—feet shoulder-width apart, knees slightly bent, and shoulders rounded and relaxed. Breathe deep and steady throughout. Begin by briskly rubbing your hands together to warm them up and activate Qi flow.

Face Washing

Lay both palms directly on your face. Gently move your hands up and down and around your face visualizing the movement of Qi in your face and throughout your whole head.

Note: *This technique will help to stimulate the epidermal layers of your skin and help to soften your skin and increase its elasticity.*

Scalp Massage

Starting at your front hairline, press all your fingertips against your scalp and push them all the way to your back hairline. Lift your fingers off your scalp, return them to your front hairline, and repeat. Be sure to move along the arc of your scalp just above your ears as well, from front to back.

Note: *There are seventeen key points where acupuncture meridians intersect on your scalp affecting everything from your motor centers in your legs to your liver. This treatment affects these points through your palpation and serves to energize the whole body.*

Ear Massage

Grab your right earlobe with your right thumb and index finger. Reach over your head with your left hand and grab the top portion of your right ear. Massage your ear, pressing firmly along the edge and inner cartilaginous parts with both hands. Gently tug your ear away from your head and longitudinally. Repeat with your left ear.

Note: *Auricular acupuncture is a system that treats the whole body solely with points on the ear. The theory is that our ear represents our whole body. The points that are mapped onto the ear can be seen by imagining an infant's curled up body superimposed on the ear, the head correlating with the ear lobe and the spine matching with the outer curve of the ear. Massaging the ear with this technique treats the whole body. It is also useful for energizing blood flow throughout the body and bringing up body temperature.*

Eye/Liver Energizing

Put your thumbs on your temples, right thumb on right temple, left on left. Curl your fingers in as if making a fist. Press the middle portion of your index fingers on the inner point of your eyebrows at the bridge of your nose. Gently and slowly slide your fingers across the eyebrows all the way to the temple. Keep your pressure even. Repeat this three times. Move the middle of your index finger to the inside corner of your eye and gently slide your fingers across the eyeball of your closed eye, all the way to your temple. Repeat this three times. Move the middle of your index finger to the inside corner of your eye, just on the orbital ridge—the bone just below your eyeball. Slide your fingers along this bone all the way to the temple. Repeat this three times.

Note: *The points around your eyes are on the Liver meridian. This treatment not only energizes your eyes and associated muscles but serves to strengthen your liver. Try this when your eyes are fatigued from overuse.*

Sinus Energizing

With your thumbs on your temples, place the middle of your index finger just beneath the inside protrusion of your cheekbone. With a strong inhalation, slide your fingers along the underside of your cheekbone all the way to your temple. Keep a firm and steady pressure. Repeat three times.

Note: *This is a great treatment when you are congested and can help to open your sinus cavity. Try it right before a strenuous physical workout to stimulate your lungs.*

Mouth/Stomach/TMJ

Using your index and middle fingers, gently rub around your lips while your mouth is open. Alternately open your mouth wide and relax. Slide your fingers along your jawline to the temporal mandibular joint (TMJ) where it attaches to your skull. Press into this indentation with your middle finger as you open and partially close your mouth.

Note: *The points around your mouth relate to your Stomach meridian so massaging this area will both help keep the skin of your face healthy and energize your stomach. Pressing into your TMJ along with deep diaphragmatic breathing will help to release blocks and tension at this important point.*

Throat/Lymph Nodes

Use the tips of your fingers to rub up and down your throat. Move them up into and along the underside of your jawline.

Note: *This is an excellent technique for energizing your lymph nodes* *and overall lymph system. Consciously manipulating the Qi along the outside of your throat can help reduce the pain of a sore throat and quicken recovery.*

Leg Stimulation

With your torso bent, firmly slap your legs. Start at the upper front portion of your thighs and slap down to your ankles. Slap the inside, outside and back of each leg.

Note: *Stimulating your legs in this way helps activate blood flow and energize Qi movement after standing in one place for a long time.*

Kidney Energizing

Make an open fist with each hand, loosening your fingers so that the tip of your index finger touches the middle of your thumb. With your hands behind your back, loosen your wrists as you hit your lumbar region near your kidneys with the thumb sides of your fists. Gently but firmly alternate hits to each kidney for about two minutes.

Note: *This exercise is a very common sight in parks across China. Though mostly associated as a treatment for the elderly, kidney energizing is valuable for people of any age. It can help with lower back pain and stress as well as stimulate Qi flow in the Kidneys and the powerful Ming Men area of the lower back.*

Rag Doll Shaking

With arms extended forward and fingers drooping, bend your knees slightly and relax your shoulders. Make your whole body vibrate by shaking every muscle and bouncing with your legs. Keep this up for one minute or so. Next, become totally relaxed, like a rag doll, and swing your right arm over your left shoulder while your left arm comes around your back and the back of your hand slaps your kidney. Repeat this as you swap arms.

Note: *This move serves to unblock stagnant Qi in the joints and generally loosen tension in muscles and tendons. Let yourself go during this exercise and imagine yourself light and liquid.*

Toss Off Stagnant Qi

The final exercise helps energize you and toss off stagnant Qi. Make tight fists at the level of your lower Dan Tian. Raise them to the level of your upper Dan Tian, inhaling deeply. In one smooth and forceful movement, throw your fists toward the Earth, opening your hands as you reach the end. As you make this "toss," really let go and exhale with a loud shout. Bring your fists up to your lower Dan Tian and in one smooth and forceful motion, throw your fists upward toward Heaven, opening your hands as you attain your uppermost reach. Do this again out to the sides. Finally, repeat this again, tossing off Qi to the Earth.

Note: *This move is designed to release stagnant Qi in the Lungs and limbs, facilitating the movement of Qi between Heaven and Earth, Yang and Yin. To get the most out of this, really let go and shout with a strong and intentional force! It is typical in parks throughout China to see hundreds of people doing this exercise each morning.*

Do what you can of these Qigong exercises daily and join the tens of millions of people around the world that benefit from this simple and ancient health-care system.

Peace.

Public Television Qigong Documentary

The following is the actual script for the one-hour Public Television documentary that I wrote and produced called *Qigong: Ancient Chinese Healing for the 21st Century*. Many people have been asking for the transcript of this program, so I thought I'd include it in this book. I've also included the translations for the interviews with the various Qigong Masters and physicians in the program. This was an incredible experience for me, one of those journeys that at once transforms your life and opens your soul. I share this with you as a resource to help give you background on the powerful healing system of Qigong. I hope it will help this book inspire you to find a health-care system that resonates with your soul.

Qigong: Ancient Chinese Healing for the 21st Century

One-Hour Program Script—56:46 min. Public Television Broadcast Version:

©1999 Garri Garripoli, Wuji Productions

Opening, On-Screen Statement

"This program is the fruit of a personal journey. I left everything safe and comfortable behind to travel across China for two years, taking only a video camera, my last finances and a deep desire to explore firsthand the roots of the healing science called Qigong. Though I have been studying this and other energy healing systems for over twenty years, I came to learn that the process of discovery never stops. I share this documentary with all who have an open mind to the wonders of the human healing potential."

Garri Garripoli, October 1998

Part 1: Introduction

As the Chinese have begun to open their cultural doors to us in the West, we have been introduced to fascinating medical alternatives such as acupuncture and herbal remedies. Now, perhaps somewhat cautiously, they are introducing another highly effective treatment system to our shores. It's called Qigong (pronounced "chee gung") and its translation to English might be simply "breath-energy exercise." This may be misleading since this treatment offers considerably more health advantages than just respiratory function. On the surface, Qigong is a healthcare modality that builds the immune system and strengthens the body through a series of slow-moving exercises performed in synchrony with deep breathing rhythms. Upon closer inspection, Qigong reveals itself to be a self-healing tool using a moving form of meditation. As we enter into a deeper dialogue with its essential philosophy, the practitioner is carried to an intimate understanding of their connection with nature, the universe and other human beings.

Realizing this connection comes through the understanding

of the essence of *Qi*, ("chee") which can be thought of as "bioelectric energy," or the vital life force that animates the human organism. According to Traditional Chinese Medicine theory, Qi is derived from the air we breathe and the food we eat . . . and can be transferred from the people and myriad living and non-living "things" we encounter in our life. Qigong is not limited to a "self"-healing system but is also a treatment method for healing, or helping to balance imbalances found in others on a body, mind and soul level. Qigong is the technique that helps us gather, store, circulate and strengthen our Qi. This improves our health by vitalizing our tissues, organs, muscles and bones—relieving pain, eliminating stress and strengthening our ability to "emit" Qi for use in healing others.

With a history that can be traced back some five thousand years, China's Qigong methodology has been around long enough to become quite apocryphal due to the fantastic healing stories that have been associated with it. In light of this, Qigong practice, along with other health and exercise approaches that may have entertained philosophical beliefs, was repressed and subsequently dropped from public awareness during the Cultural Revolution. In the new and more open China, the thousands of medical Qigong healing claims, from hypertension to cancer, challenges Western credibility. As a result, even the youth culture of China is more than a little skeptical of this ancient and mysterious approach to health and spiritual well-being.

This program looks at the fascinating healthcare system of Qigong, first through the eyes of history, exploring both its religious and cultural evolution, and then through the eyes of some contemporary Qigong Masters. Through interviews with respected Chinese medical doctors who have researched Qigong, we will see how the current trend in searching for an effective, low-cost health-care strategy is helping to create a place for Qigong in our future—a future that puts healthcare back in the hands of the individual.

Part 2: The Chinese Medical Perspective

Not all Chinese accept the claims of Qigong on face value. To some it is simply an antiquated practice based on superstitious beliefs, and in a country that is rapidly embracing things Western, the old is being discarded at an alarming rate. In what may seem counter to this trend, teams of Western-trained medical doctors are taking a serious look at the potential for Qigong to play a vital role in the increasingly demanding health-care needs of the world's most populous country.

In the heart of Shanghai, China's largest city and powerful financial and trade center, two medical physicians have been working for three decades to methodically and scientifically show the efficacy of Qigong for treating hypertension. At the Shanghai Institute of Hypertension, Drs. Wang and Shu have amassed the most thoroughly tested and credible data on the positive effects that the practice of Qigong has on people suffering from high blood pressure. Their work is so extensive that they have tracked some people for over thirty years.

Dr. Wang and Dr. Shu statements:

> "Our research results show that the effectiveness of Qigong is very positive."
>
> "Our physicians prescribe herbs, lifestyle changes and then various Qigong exercises."
>
> "We saw that blood pressure was controlled and quality of life went up."
>
> "According to traditional Chinese medicine, different people and different symptoms require different Qigong exercises."
>
> "But all Qigong systems have three common aspects—regulation of the posture for relaxation, regulation of the mind and regulation of breathing."
>
> "We think Qigong can cure every kind of disease, some responding better than others."

Across town at the Shanghai Qigong Institute, government-funded research has been going on for many years to discover how Qigong can be successfully incorporated into the country's social healthcare system. Dr. Sheng Kang Yi not only studies Qigong from a renowned Master who lives in the mountains far from town, but works long days putting his findings to use in the clinic at the Institute.

Dr. Sheng Kang Yi statement:

> "The only thing we can research now is the effects of Qigong on patients since no device can measure 'Qi.' We compare groups treated with and without Qigong

and we see very positive results. It is this kind of research that will help Westerners believe. A lot of diseases can be successfully treated by Qigong. . . . If they see the results, they will know."

Up North in Beijing, the capital and cultural center of the country, Dr. Wu Jin, a Western-trained physician who is also a Qigong practitioner, heads up research at the Xi Yuan Hospital. Though we weren't allowed to shoot at her facility because of security reasons, Dr. Wu shares her groundbreaking work:

Dr. Wu Jin translation:

"After working for years with many, many patients at the hospital, we have conclusive evidence that Qigong can assist in treatment and recovery of nearly every disease. Postoperative recovery time was shortened dramatically in patients who used Qigong over patients who employed standard Western techniques."

In Purple Bamboo Park, hidden amidst the hustle and bustle of Beijing, a loyal group of terminally ill cancer patients has formed a "club" as they call it. Frustrated by the hopelessness they felt from their Western-trained physicians, they follow a technique of "walking Qigong" developed by the late Dr. Guo Lin in hopes of reversing their illness. Master Liu Shu Hua, a master in this system, learned directly from Mrs. Guo Lin who developed this walking technique from several ancient systems. Suffering from urogenital cancer and told she would only have a few weeks left to live, Dr. Guo Lin lived twenty more healthy years, devoting her life to giving hope to cancer patients. These club members have all outlived their own terminal diagnoses by many years.

Part 3: Qigong History

The actual word "Qigong" was only coined in 1962, but the principles upon which it is based are found in records thousands of years old. In an ancient tomb, these items were buried in hopes that the deceased, a wealthy nobleman, would have good health in the afterlife. This tortoise shell has survived nearly three thousand years to tell us through its ancient inscriptions that people of that time believed deep breathing and specific stretching exercises would infuse them with the energy of Qi and keep them healthy and vital. These drawings, dated to be about twenty-five hundred years old, show ancient "Dao Yin" movements. They were part of a stylized tribal dance that helped alleviate aches and pains, presumably from rheumatoid arthritis that was common with workers in the rice paddies and in other damp conditions. These dances were eventually broken down into specific moves that were "prescribed" for different ailments. Another way that the principles of deep breathing and mobilizing internal energy was applied was in the area of military battle. Systems like Wuji Qigong trace their origins to secret techniques and exercises coveted by warriors to make them better soldiers.

At the Shaolin Temple, the revered fifteen-hundred-year-old

Buddhist stronghold in Henan Province, the gentle monks eventually became known across the nation for their extraordinary skills in battle. Originally, this Ch'an sect of Buddhists—we are more familiar with its Japanese branch known as Zen—lived ascetic lives and consumed their time in deep, sedentary meditation on the Buddha—and a Qigong that focused on building a strong spirit.

Shaolin Buddhist Master Monk statements:

"The average man thinks of so many things; he must sit and not think of anything if he is to be truly healthy."

"If you're sick, don't think of it or identify with it, sit and meditate, relax, take your mind off the sickness . . ."

"Everything belongs to Qigong . . . if I return to the natural time and world, I will be free . . . just like a point has three world coordinates; if I am free, I can move into unlimited time and space . . ."

In 515 A.D., the Indian holyman Bodhi Dharma happened upon the Temple after a long journey. He climbed to the top of Song Mountain, and for nine years remained in seclusion inside a cave. When he emerged, he began to teach the Shaolin monks a complete system of movement based on the way animals move in nature. He frowned on their sitting Qigong meditation, speaking of how "Qi" became stagnant and how this would lead inevitably to ill health. His animal-inspired movements became the foundation of the Shaolin Kung Fu fighting style that brought notoriety and political favor to the temple, helping it to survive all these years. It's important to note that the core of the fighting techniques lies in the Qigong breathing and Qi energy-focusing principles. Bodhi Dharma, coming from India, brought ancient Hindu Yoga techniques with him and it is easy to see how some of these premises are incorporated into Chinese Qigong. Literally thousands of Qigong styles and systems developed over the millennia. Some styles evolved into formalized routines that have become commonly known as Tai Chi.

Qigong is considered the core of both Tai Chi and the martial arts, as its fundamental premise is to use the breath to focus and mobilize energy throughout the body.

Another influence on the development of Qigong in China was Taoism. Taoism is an ancient philosophical belief system with roots that go back thousands of years to the writings of the Chinese sage named Lao-tzu. Lao-tzu and followers such as Chuang Tsu, lived in a time of great social unrest in China. They promoted a balanced lifestyle that adhered to the laws of nature. Observing the world around them, Taoists believed that their actions should harmonize with nature, reflecting the way water flows gently around obstructions or the way willows bend in the breeze. Their ceremonies honor various spirits and guardians who are infused with supernatural powers. Watching the activities of animals and celestial bodies would not only become their inspiration for living a virtuous life, but would serve to create a whole style of

Qigong that focused on balance and building a strong body.

Da Yan Qigong, a Taoist style performed here by Master Fan Fu Xing of Xi'an, is named after the big wild goose and its forms reflect the natural movements of this beautiful bird. As the goose is a symbol of longevity, Master Fan says that this system will bring the practitioner good health and a long life. Over one million Chinese currently practice this four-hundred-year-old Qigong system.

Buddhism and Taoism are considered the two pillars that support the philosophy of the Chinese people. It is curious that they in fact complement each other and their combined influence works together to create a complete way of thinking that has molded the evolution of Qigong over the millennia.

Qigong is more than a set of exercises, it is an attitude that works to restructure one's perspective on life, leading to balance and harmony with the world around us.

Part 4: The Cultural Revolution

As the Tao teaches, life is an ever-changing process. The beginning of this century saw China in a state of moral and social decay, civil infighting and eventually, war with Japan. The hope for a unified and stronger country led to the Cultural Revolution, which would dramatically force people to re-evaluate their traditional way of life. Ancient traditional practices such as Qigong, which were feared as old-fashioned and religious superstitions, were outlawed and forced underground until only recently. Many Masters left the mainland, as did the nationalist leader Chiang Kai-shek, and a rather hurried exodus took place across the Taiwan Straits. For others less fortunate, the practice of this ancient healing system stopped altogether as intellectuals, monks and professionals were persecuted and forced into hard labor on farms and in factories.

When the Cultural Revolution came to an end in 1976, China once again opened its doors to the West and to its own cultural past. Interestingly enough, it was also Mao Tse Tung who instigated research on Qigong to test its viability. Evidence was overwhelming that this health-care modality would actually be a great benefit to the people. Its easy-to-learn techniques and ability to maintain health at such a low cost brought it to great favor in a country with over one billion people, and a government responsible for socialized medical care.

For this reason, Qigong has continued to be heavily researched and promoted by the government of the People's Republic of China.

Part 5: Master Duan

The traditional method of learning Qigong is from a Master—a teacher who has the experience to impart both the subtleties of their particular system as well as the "Qi" or energy necessary to infuse the student with the "unspoken" teachings. One of these great elder masters is

Duan Zhi Liang. He has lived most of his ninety years in Beijing. His teacher, in keeping with tradition, was his grandfather. His father was a guard at the Forbidden City as were his grandfather and great-grandfather, who were both doctors. While they protected the last emperor, young Duan played in the courtyard and learned the ways of a warrior. The Duan family holds the lineage for the Wuji style of Qigong, which dates back to the eighth century as noted on this ancient tablet now located at the Confucian school in Xi'an. The tablet, known as the Da Qin Jing Jiao, was discovered along the Silk Road and records the interactions between the Chinese and Christians traveling from the West. Master Duan, like his family, is a devout Catholic and his unique form of Qigong encompasses the Taoist and Buddhist beliefs as well as Christian principles. Although Qigong is not a religion and requires no change in belief system to practice, it is common that the balance and peace one feels after doing these exercises will extend to all aspects of one's life. Master Duan, who has been studying Wuji Qigong and martial arts since he was seven years old, is a doctor of Traditional Chinese Medicine who is renowned for his compassion and generosity.

He typically charges ten Yuan, which is about one U.S. dollar, for a Qigong treatment. Master Duan incorporates acupuncture, moxibustion and tui'na massage techniques with his Wuji Qigong. This means he uses his own "wei Qi" or emitted energy to help balance the imbalances in his patients. It is believed that these energy imbalances lead to all illnesses and ailments. As with all great Qigong masters, the power of their balanced Qi and what they collect from nature actually catalyzes and promotes balance and healing in their patients.

To build up his own Qi and to maintain his health and internal physical and mental balance, Master Duan practices Wuji Qigong for one hour each morning, usually starting at 5 or 6 A.M. This is followed by a strenuous Kung Fu workout where this ninety-year-old Master routinely spars with other Masters and students one-third his age.

Master Duan's Wuji Qigong is an easy-to-learn system that is comprised of eighteen individual forms. Each form is designed to energize different internal organs and promote Qi energy flow throughout the body. Stretching in various ways both loosens the muscles and tendons while stimulating the twelve acupuncture meridians. This helps to unblock stagnant Qi, believed to be the root of physical and mental problems. Wuji Qigong has its roots in sword fighting, the Duan family specialty. Many of the moves are focused on loosening up and strengthening the shoulders, neck and wrists—keys to winning in battle—and coincidentally key trouble spots for modern-day computer users.

Curiously, Master Duan believes one cannot be a good fighter without being a good healer, so his emphasis is equally put on both. On the battleground, a warrior must be adept at tending to his own wounds and those of his fellow soldiers. The powerful techniques of Qigong were thus coveted as secret knowledge since holding this information meant having the competitive edge.

Even with his deep honor of traditional ways, Master Duan's magic lies in his incredible flexibility. His openness to new ideas and willingness to grow and learn is what he says keeps him young at heart. It is also the essence of his Qigong teaching.

Master Duan believes that practicing the slow and specific moves of Qigong helps us to remember that we are all connected through a singular, infinite energy he calls Wuji ("woo jee"). He believes that understanding the concept of chaos in nature will help us with all we encounter:

Master Duan statement:

> *"The essence of all evolution in nature emerges from chaos. By understanding the infinite energy that is always available to us, we can flow naturally with the chaotic rhythms of the Universe. Try to avoid patterns and repetition, mix things up and let Qi flow smoothly . . . remain flexible and relaxed in all you do. This is truly to understand Qigong."*

Experiencing the deep and synchronized breathing of Qigong, he says, connects us to the original breath that created the Universe.

A true Master, Duan Zhi Liang is consumed with his passion. He teaches constantly at parks around the city and has recently started teaching foreign doctors. His wife of forty-five years works with him, as she is also a well-respected teacher and healer. The balance of his time is spent treating patients at one of his two simple Qigong clinics located in impoverished neighborhoods in Beijing. He chooses to share his vast knowledge with a wonderful sense of humor and joy.

Part 6: Master Luo

On the outskirts of Beijing is a unique clinic specializing in "bone setting," or what we may think of as a combination of chiropractic and physical therapy. It's a family-run business founded by the ninety-two-year-old Master Luo, the matriarch of a healing dynasty that spans five generations. With dozens of family members, and her son as the clinic director—a Western-trained physician as well as a Qigong Master himself—Master Luo practices a unique style of Qigong that focuses on using Qi in conjunction with subtle bone manipulations to cure a variety of physical problems. With ailments ranging from common emergencies arising from bicycle accidents to various chronic pain syndromes, an average of eighty patients come to this little clinic each day. Master Luo charges a dollar or two per treatment and still uses the same little stick to transmit Qi as she has for the past seventy years. Since the age of ten, her life has been based on a devotion to helping people in pain:

Master Luo statement:

> *"One must do good for the country, for others . . . it keeps you healthy and young."*

"Some patients are rich, some are poor, but you must treat them the same way."

"Everything I do is for the good of the people."

By focusing her Qi and her healing intention through her stick, or sometimes her thumb, she is able to ease pain, realign spines and reset dislocated bones and joints.

Master Luo statement:

"I have a very experienced thumb. I've used my big finger for more than seventy years . . . it's very important."

"If you invite me to America to teach, I only have to bring my thumb!"

This clinic has an X-ray machine, which each doctor uses for diagnosis. Many Western techniques are used to complement Qigong here. Dr. Luo is proud to speak of the way this clinic is open to all means that will help make their patients heal faster. He was curious about our IBM laptop and thought it could be an excellent educational tool. The open-mindedness of the Luo family, like many Qigong doctors in China, is part of their great gift. They combine artistry and a deep love of their culture to enhance their ability to heal. Dr. Luo is expert at Tai Chi swords which helps him to build and balance his internal Qi. He enjoys discussing the value of combining Qigong with clinical treatments:

Dr. Luo statement:

"If Western medicine is best, we use those techniques. If Eastern is correct, we use that."

"The Chinese have a proverb, 'It is better not to use a knife when trying to heal someone.'"

"Surgery causes much discomfort in a patient—we don't use it unless it's necessary."

"Qigong is useful in treatment and in reducing recovery time. Traditional Chinese medicine says that if the acupuncture meridians move slowly, then things are not well, the patient gets painful sensations. Qi must move through the meridians smoothly in order to heal and this theory applies to bone-related diseases as well."

At the core of the Luo family philosophy is the desire to help others. Master Luo doesn't like to even talk about Qi or the principles of Qigong and how it works. She would rather speak of intention and where one's heart needs to be:

Master Luo statements:

"The force from the heart can do many things."
"Many forces come from the inside, not only physical strength."
"I may be ninety-two, but I'm still very forceful."
"We must do good things for the people, nothing bad, this is a socialist country after all . . ."

To Master Luo, Qigong is a process of acting from a pure heart, of caring about others and visualizing wholeness and good health. . . . She is an example of charity and compassion and revered for both her own healing powers and the Qigong techniques that she has passed on to her family and students so that others can live a better life.

Part 7: Master Wan

A student of both Master Duan and Master Luo is Dr. Wan Su Jian, a unique example of the new generation of Qigong masters to emerge in modern China. At forty-three years old, Master Wan has been studying Qigong and traditional Chinese medicine for thirty-six years. His mother is a renowned acupuncturist in Da Tong, a coal-mining city far in the North of the country. His father, a retired director of a large, government-run Western hospital, now assists his wife in their clinic, naturally combining Western procedures with traditional acupuncture. They are proud of their son, who they set on his path to become a healer when he was only seven, and who is now considered one of the most well-respected Qigong doctors in the country.

Master Wan statement:

> *"People come here from all over the world for treatment, sometimes nearly dying. How great it is that we can take ideas from the Chinese traditional I Ching and Bagua that are thousands of years old and use them to keep us in good health today. We must continue to do research though to constantly improve on the past."*

In his own clinic and training facility nestled in the hills at the edge of Beijing, Master Wan has created a learning environment where young students can take up Qigong as a vocational skill and bring it into the work force. Some forty students at a time are under his tutelage, following the age-old tradition of learning from a master— but with the added practicality of job placement. The prerequisite for these students is three years of study at the Shaolin Temple where their strenuous, round-the-clock training brings them discipline and the fundamentals of Qigong and Kung Fu. As many of the students arrive here at the age of fifteen, it means their family sent them to Shaolin at the age of eleven or twelve, taking them out of their traditional schooling and into this live-in learning environment.

What these young people lack in geometry and science, they more than make up with practical medical training and an inner strength, humbleness and confidence that one rarely sees in this generation.

Master Wan, a father himself with the state limit of one child, is a born leader. He has served thirty years in the Red Army, rising high in the ranks while pursuing his medical career. His strength in Qigong brought him notoriety and freedom within the military establishment to pursue his work. After being given his own military Qigong hospital, he has now created this unique training facility where patients from all over the world are treated. He and his students routinely treat high government officials and powerful businesspeople as their reputation as healers continues to rise.

Master Wan combines an ancient Taoist Qigong system called Bagua Xun Tao Gong ("Bagwa shun dao gung") with Traditional Chinese Medicine procedures to achieve his great success with paralysis, cancer patients and a wide variety of diseases. This system of Qigong utilizes the practitioner's emitted "Wei Qi" to affect the Qi field of the patient. The patient's energy is considered "out of balance," some symptoms suggesting their Qi is weak or in other cases, excessive. The Qigong practitioner helps to restore a healthy balance by moving their hands in a specific way around the patient.

It is believed that everyone has a "Qi field" around and through them; the proper manipulation of this field is a step in the process of healing. This manipulation is done by the passing of the practitioner's hand through this field and helping to bring about a shift and restructuring of Qi while infusing them with Qi from nature. Some practitioners seem to have better success than others and Master Wan's unique style of having several Qigong doctors working on a single patient has proven to bring about profound and lasting results.

He continually explores new techniques, like these electrically stimulated acupuncture needles, and combines them with his emitted Qi treatments. Like all Qigong Masters, Dr. Wan practices inner and outer exercises to replenish and strengthen his Qi. This applies to his students as well, and the strenuous regimen he puts them through has helped to create a powerful team of young Qigong Masters. He constantly lectures on the importance of this self-discipline, not only for the practitioner, but also for the patient. A major key in successful Qigong healing is follow-up practice by the patient after their treatment, and is what he attributes to his high success rate. Japanese patients arrive by the dozens and have created rehabilitation groups where they practice Qigong exercises after they return home from their weeklong treatment.

As a Taoist, Master Wan's Qigong training emphasizes a connection with nature, gathering Yin Qi from the Earth and Yang Qi from the sky. He teaches that this balance of Yin and Yang from the Universe around us reflects the inner balance that we need in order to heal. Healing in the Qigong philosophy is not only of the body, but also of the mind and spirit. These three aspects of our nature are inseparable and thus must be treated as a coherent whole.

Like Master Duan and Master Luo, Master Wan lives by the philosophy that compassion and virtue are the keys to a healthy life and to success as a healer. Money should never be a motivating force as it will only weaken your Qi. They all believe that if one follows the path of a virtuous life and a life of balance, you will be provided for in ways that are best suited for your unfolding and growth.

Part 8: Cultural Technology

Qigong has also captured the interest of the scientific community. Their hope is to somehow quantify Qi, to break it down into some definable elements and then regenerate it. The leading pioneer in this area is Lu Yan

Fang, affectionately known as Engineer Lu. Her ground-breaking work at the Electro-Acoustical Research Institute is well-respected around the world. Fifteen years ago, Engineer Lu had the idea that the Qi emissions from Qigong Masters could be somehow measured acoustically. In the Institute's anechoic chamber, she suspended a highly sensitive microphone near the "Lao Gong" point in their palms, the traditional acupressure point where healing Qi is emitted. Upon demand, these Masters could emit a low-frequency audio signal in the eight- to fourteen-hertz range. It was a chaotic signal with an ever-changing pattern. She tested many average adults who showed no such pattern but did find that young children exhibited similar audio emissions. The result of this research was the development of the Qigong Machine, a hand-held device that actually replicates this audio portion of the Qi emission.

Co-developed and marketed by China Healthways in San Clemente, California, this device is used by thousands of physicians and chiropractors in the United States. Testimonials of chronic pain relief, energy boosting and the reduction of swelling from sprains are numerous.

Although Qi is considered by authorities to be a more complex radiation than just an audio wave form, the Qigong Machine is an example of what may lie ahead as we take Qigong more seriously and delve deeper into the mysterious nature of Qi.

Part 9: Western Expert Kenneth Sancier

Hundreds of researchers throughout China have taken the task of exploring the effects of Qigong in the field of medicine. Applying scientific research methods in order to obtain results on the healing properties of Qi has its challenges, but is leading us to a deeper understanding of this elusive force. Dr. Kenneth Sancier, President and founder of the Qigong Institute in Menlo Park, California, is considered one of the foremost authorities on this field of research. Now retired from his thirty-five-year tenure as Director of SRI, the Stanford Research Institute, his deep respect by the international scientific community brings credibility and objectivity to Qigong research:

Dr. Sancier interview:

"We need to look to China to find out what kind of research is going on. Since the 1980s, a huge amount of research has been reported, but that literature is mainly in Chinese, so in order to make that information accessible to the Western people, the Qigong Institute put together a computerized Qigong database which permits people to search with any key word for a disease, or any other condition. There are about thirteen hundred references in that database.

"There's been research done showing that emitted Qi from a Qigong Master will increase the rate of growth of seedlings, mushrooms. It will affect brain waves of anesthesized animals and many different things that can be done that don't depend exclusively on psychological elements.

"Qigong is a therapy for chronic conditions primarily, although not exclusively, whereas Western medicine is primarily for acute conditions like surgery or bacterial infections and so forth.

"The Western and Eastern approaches can be worked together and should be complementary because they're dealing with different aspects of healing."

Part 10. Current Qigong Situation Around China and Tibet

Most of the exploration into the healing powers of Qigong is going on outside of the laboratories. In parks throughout China, literally millions of people practice Qigong each day. One can witness the myriad styles in any town and province you visit. Though we may think that the therapeutic aspects of this healthcare system might only be achieved through rigorous exercise movements, some styles involve simply sitting, while many would rather apply it to what looks like traditional dancing. Here in Shanghai, hundreds of couples come to the waterfront each morning to practice their Qigong as dance. A thousand miles away in Luo Yang, massive crowds dance their Qigong to the guidance of a Master instructor.

Another aspect of Qigong lies within the Tai Chi swordplay. Like Master Duan and Master Wan, they use the metal in the sword to help absorb Qi into their bodies.

Most people may not think of calligraphy as Qigong,

but several Master artists are renowned for the healing powers that they impart through their artwork. It is believed that their powerful Qi is passed into the finished piece and can benefit those who view it. Master Liu of Cheng Du, an ancient city near the Tibetan border of China, is eighty-four years old and well-respected for his Qigong calligraphy and swordplay. He sees the paintbrush and the sword as one and the same, since it is in fact one's Qi that is animating them both. His grace and elegance are the reflection of the refined Qi that he has cultivated over years of study. At Master Zhang Yuan Ming's Heavenly Dragon Temple, loyal students are taught the subtle aspects of strengthening and applying Qi to all they do.

Across the country at the Shi Fan Yuan temple, Master Sun Ming Rui creates beautiful artwork while in a deep Qigong meditation. A Taoist monk, he lives an austere life in this mountaintop retreat. He says that he never had any artistic tendencies until late in his eighty-year life. One day, after doing years of Qigong in one of the temple's gardens, he said he "saw" the essence of the flowers in that moment and deeply understood his connection to them. He picked up a paintbrush for the first time and began to paint. His art is now considered a national treasure and each piece he finishes is carefully wrapped and shipped to an official caretaker in Beijing.

This Taoist temple is typical in that all of the monks are trained to apply their Qigong to creative outlets. All of the monks or "Daoshi" (dao-sha) are vegetarian musicians.

They play traditional Taoist temple music in a heightened Qigong state, thus imparting to the listener the strength and healing balance of their Qi. Amongst them is a small group who have been trained since childhood to develop their Qi in order to perform extraordinary physical feats. Much like the Shaolin monks with their acts of supreme skill, these young men focus much of their waking energy to mastering techniques that defy physics. Breaking stones with their bare hands, withstanding rigorous physical tests and performing feats of balance under challenging conditions is part of their Qigong training. By learning to build their *wei Qi* ("way chee") or "protective Qi," they are able to strengthen their bodies in order to master these skills. These extreme feats serve to inspire others to practice even basic Qigong techniques for self-healing and general well-being.

In Tibet, Qigong seems to be incorporated into the very fabric of daily life for these gentle Buddhists. When we think of this country, we are reminded of the austere life of the monks who live in the few remaining temples throughout this magical land. Their Qigong is practiced in prayer, mostly performed in silence or with gentle chanting. For the Tibetans, the use of repetitive sounds or mantras is key to obtaining the healing benefits of Qigong.

The average Tibetan journeys to a temple each week and walks around and around it, chanting a specific mantra. Coming on horseback or by foot for miles along severe terrain, the Tibetan knows the value of this walking Qigong practice. To these spiritual people, every moment of every day is an opportunity to honor life, to appreciate the beauty and power of the Universe, and to accept all that comes to them with an open and loving heart.

Within China, like all growing, industrialized countries, there is a major concern about managing the health-care needs of the citizens. As in the West, rising health-care costs are presenting a tremendous financial burden on valuable limited resources. The Chinese government has been looking seriously at the possibility of Qigong to relieve some of this pressure.

Deep in Hebei Province, Master Zhi Chen Guo has been developing a Qigong style that he feels is actually tran-scending what we know as Qigong. His system is known as *Zhi Neng* ("juh nung") Medicine and combines Qigong with both Traditional Chinese Medicine and Western medi-cal theory. What makes this system so profound is that two million loyal students practice it regularly and claim in-credible results. At his sanitorium and treatment center, an eleven-hundred bed clinic is combined with an herbal pharmacy and training center capable of handling five thousand students at one time. The select students that are invited to come here travel by bicycle and bus from around China to learn in person from Master Guo. They believe his Qi energy, combined with the various exercises they perform for hours at a time, help in their training and healing. The fact is that many come here to heal them-selves from all forms of disease.

Guo's system involves both Qigong exercises and various herb combinations that he prescribes just by glancing at the patient, using his unique skills. With his team of doctors he is able to treat hundreds of people a day at his clinic. This low-cost and effective system is exactly what the government is looking for and therefore allows this individual to build such a following.

Many Zhi Neng Medicine support groups are growing around the country and are overseen by local government agencies that are proud of the initiative and self-responsibility individuals are taking to maintain their health.

Master Guo is now hoping to share Zhi Neng Medicine with Westerners. To this end, he has selected a renowned Chinese medical doctor to be his representative in the West. This man, Dr. Zhi Gang Sha, is both a Western-trained physician as well as a traditional Chinese doctor who has taught in Beijing at the World Health Organization's International Medical Center. Dr. Sha, a Qigong Master who began his training at the age of seven, is now the adopted son of Master Guo and has been given the responsibility of spreading the healing power of Zhi Neng Medicine to the West. Dr. Sha has moved to Canada and has recently visited America to begin this process of teaching what he and Master Guo feel will be the force of self-healing for the twenty-first century. The system utilizes hand positioning to help move Qi to unblock stagnation that causes chronic pain. Combined with this are various mantras that are believed to activate Qi movement in specific parts of the body. For difficult cases, he uses a unique form of acupuncture that utilizes only twelve acupoints. Dr. Sha inserts the needles very quickly but says he uses his Qi to enhance the healing effects.

The claims of his healing abilities and those of the various Zhi Neng Medicine techniques grow daily, and Western physicians are beginning to take a serious look at how these new healing modalities may eventually complement Western medicine.

Part 11: Conclusion

Qigong, a five-thousand-year-old healing modality, has evolved and adapted itself to the times, and has been molded by its various teachers. Like every system in life, there are bad teachers and good teachers, those with little integrity and those who are gifted. Although thousands of different styles have emerged over the millennia, the common threads that tie sincere proponents of this healing system together remain the same.

The first key is the breath. Every form of Qigong puts great emphasis on deep, diaphragmatic breathing. Though there may be many techniques and unique ways to manipulate the breath, the fact remains that if one can find time throughout the day to devote some attention to focused yet relaxed deep-breathing, they will experience a certain level of benefit. For some this may mean relaxation. As relaxation relieves the body of additional stress, the immune system has less work to do and more energy can be devoted to staying healthy. Super-oxygenating the body through intentional deep breathing will also supply the body with more of the fuel it needs to repair and maintain health.

The second key is slow and gentle movement and stretching. With physical flexibility comes mental flexibility. When deep breath is combined with slow, synchronized movement, the body builds more energy or Qi rather than depleting energy, which happens with strenuous exercise. When the body moves with the breath, many people experience a sense of calm and harmony. This sensation helps to bring the body and mind into balance and contributes to our physical and mental healing.

Qigong is not tied to any religious belief system. Although it has been influenced over the millennia by much philosophical thought, people from all walks of life practice Qigong, since it is free of dogma. It is common that practitioners experience both a deep sense of calm and increased vitality. Many say it has changed the way they look at life—as if their senses have been awakened.

Many authorities agree that healing is heavily influenced by one's state of mind. It is thought that if a person is more positive and at ease, they will successfully contribute to their own healing. Qigong appears to have the potential of being a simple technique that can be learned by anyone and provides tangible results that even scientists can quantify. Of great interest to all is that practicing Qigong can cut down hospitalization time and cost, reduce the amount of medication one needs during con-valescence, and promote healing in diseases ranging from hypertension to cancer. In a word, Qigong has the potential of drastically reducing the cost of healthcare.

Most importantly, Qigong offers a way for individuals to take responsibility for their own health, and to alleviate the sense of helplessness that often exists in today's healthcare system.

With healthcare costs skyrocketing and health management programs reducing choice and availability, Qigong is presenting the opportunity for motivated people to be more involved in their own physical, mental and spiritual health. Qigong is a powerful complement to our current healing modalities. It is an ancient Chinese healing system that honors the past and provides the tools that can enable us to truly help others and ourselves as we enter the twenty-first century.

Part 12: Credits

My deepest gratitude to all my friends throughout China, Tibet and America, from Masters to military, who have entered my heart and soul and without whom this project would not have been possible.

For further information contact:

Garri Garripoli

Wuji Productions

c/o Conscious Wave

360 Interlocken Boulevard, Suite 300

Broomfield, CO 80021

www.WujiProductions.com

Glossary

The following is a list of words that will assist you in understanding this book and others about the subject of Qigong. It is by no means a complete list of Qigong terminology, but simply a helpful way to get a grasp on certain concepts that are fundamental to this practice. Note that when the names of organs are capitalized throughout this book, they refer to the acupuncture meridian energy system associated with that organ and not the organ specifically. Please remember that most of these words refer to theoretical and symbolic ideas that should not be misconstrued as actual physical locations. Though they refer to spots in the body, they are better thought of as "energy centers." Looking at them from more of a metaphorical perspective will help you to understand the true essence behind each concept.

Ba Gua. "Eight Directions"—the eight sacred points on the compass and is literally used as a reference to the Earth and all things on the physical plane. As this is a Taoist concept, making reference to nature refers to all things that were created from the joining of Yin and Yang forces in the Universe. The symbol of the Ba Gua is depicted as eight trigrams, symbolizing the various energetic aspects of life as outlined in the I Ching.

Bai Hui Point. "Point of 100 Reasons"—the acupressure point on the crown of the head known as Du 20. A key point in Qigong practice, it is believed that this point can be opened in order to receive Universal Qi, thought information, and Yang Qi.

Jing. Though there is no English translation, Jing is thought of as the prenatal Qi. We receive this at birth as it is passed down from our parents. It is associated with the past, sexuality and the Kidney System.

Lao Gong Point. "Hard Working Point"—the acupressure point in the middle of the palm known as Pericardium 8. A key point in Qigong practice believed to be the most powerful spot in the body for emitting Qi.

Lower Dan Tian. "Lower Elixir Field"—located below the navel, this is the central gathering point of Qi and one of three "Dan Tian" regions in the body. During Qigong practice, it is advised that our focus be directed to this point for strengthening Jing Qi and for an overall centering of our being.

Meridian. Known in Mandarin as the "Jing Luo,"

meridian refers to the acupuncture channels that run throughout the body. As most are associated with organ systems, points along the meridians are used to treat illnesses and other imbalances. Though Qi flows freely throughout the body in a healthy person, it travels in a most direct way through the twelve main, and numerous minor, meridians. An acupuncture textbook can show you illustrations of these pathways.

Middle Dan Tian. "Middle Elixir Field"—located in the center of the chest, it is an important gathering point of Qi and one of three "Dan Tian" regions in the body. Associated with the heart center, Shen Qi is thought to be best attracted here, along with the upper Dan Tian.

Ming Men. "Life Gate"—the acupressure point in the middle of the lower back known as Du 4. This point is considered a portal for Jing Qi as it is associated with the Kidneys and is opposite the lower Dan Tian. Sensing an "opening" or feeling at this point is considered a high-level achievement in Qigong practice.

Nei Qi. "Inner Qi"—this is the Qi that moves within our bodies, flowing through our meridians, veins, arteries, muscles, bones, etc.

Qi. There is no direct translation that suffices, though it literally means "air." Qi is the energy that animates all life. It exists everywhere as a form of radiation similar to heat and sound, yet much more complex. We generate new Qi from the food we eat, the air we breathe, and the energy we absorb from people, thoughts and things we encounter every day.

Shen. "Spirit"—this is a type of Qi that is associated with our Spirit body. It facilitates our mental capacity and thus our imagination and creativity. Shen is linked to future energy.

Tao. One translation is "the way," as in the way of nature and the natural order. Another translation is "path." It refers to the concept that the Taoists, who recognize their teacher to be Lao-tzu, feel cannot be described. It can only be lived.

Taoism. An ancient philosophy of China attributed to the sage Lao-tzu who lived around 600 B.C. His followers, the Taoists, believed that one should live in accordance with the Tao and that the dynamic forces of Yin and Yang governed all of life.

Upper Dan Tian. "Upper Elixir Field"—located in the center of the skull, it is an important gathering point of Qi and one of three "Dan Tian" regions in the body. Associated with the pineal gland and third eye, Shen Qi moves freely here. Focalizing on this point is thought to aid in gathering with Shen Qi and reinforcing our connection with the Universe.

Wei Qi. "External Qi"—this is the Qi that exists immediately around our body and is considered as an extension of our immune system. It is our protective energy field that can deflect disease, and with practice, can aid in self-defense. It can also be referred to as "emitted Qi" as is used in the healing process.

Wu Xing. "Deep Understanding"—the complete comprehension of an idea. It is usually associated with a sense that one's whole being has been transformed in the process.

Wu Wei. "Without Effort." The concept that force should not be met with resistance. It reminds us to flow and overcome hardness with softness, negativity with positivity.

Wuji. "Without Limits" or "The End of Non-Beingness"—an ancient concept that refers to the infinite, singular consciousness of the Universe. It is believed that Yin and Yang emerged from the unity of Wuji. All things physical thus emerged from Yin and Yang. Sometimes considered to be the transition between beingness and non-beingness, the transformation of non-matter into matter, concept into creation.

Yin. The dark, cool, sedentary, feminine, nurturing aspect of nature. Associated with form, Yin is the complement of Yang while at the same time, contains it.

Yang. The light, warm, active, masculine, forceful aspect of nature. Associated with formlessness, Yang is the complement of Yin while at the same time, contains it.

Qigong Resources

This chapter will give you ways to contact many of the people who have participated in this book. It is my hope that you will follow your heart and see where it leads you. The path of discovery begins when you have the courage to make the next step. I know that each of these people are open to your questions and inquiry. Enjoy the journey.

Michiko Iwao

ADDRESS: Director
            Association of Relaxation
            Therapy, International
            (ARTI)
            11-2-4-C, Shimogyobu-cho
            Uzumasa
            Ukyo-ku, Kyoto, Japan
            616-8104

PHONE: +81-75-861-3694
FAX: +81-75-861-3719
EMAIL: *iwao@mtf.biglobe.ne.jp*

Wan Su Jian

ADDRESS: Executive Director
              Qigong Research Institute
              Shaojiapo A3rd
              Shijingshan District
              Beijing, China 100041
PHONE: 86 10-6884-9330
FAX: 86 10-6884-9329 and 86 10-6887-9254
EMAIL: *wansjian@public.east.cn.net*
BOOKS: *Ba Gua Xun Dao Gong*
              Clinical Practice of Qigong
   Qigong Master and physician

Zhang Yuan Ming

ADDRESS: International Institute for the Research of
              Traditional Science and Culture (I.T.S.C.)
              11217 Rabitisha
              Tehachapi, California 93561
PHONE: (805) 823-9341
FAX: (949) 494-7864
EMAIL: *pratpryor@aol.com*

Master Zhang is Dean of the Qigong and Acupuncture Departments of Peking Guangming Chinese Medicine

College and is the consultant to the United Nations Qigong Society. He has published a series of Medical Qigong Kung Fu videos in the United States.

Lily Sioux

ADDRESS: Tai Hsuan School of Taoist Arts
             P.O. Box 11126
             Honolulu, Hawaii 96828
PHONE: (800) 942-4788 / (808) 947-4788 (o) /
             373-2849 Sanctuary
FAX: (808) 947-1152
EMAIL: *taihsuan@acupuncture.hi.com*

Master Sioux runs a TCM clinic in Honolulu and maintains a Taoist sanctuary outside of town where, as a Qigong Master, she teaches classes here, in China and around the world.

Jerry Alan Johnson, Ph.D., D.T.C.M., D.M.Q. (China)

ADDRESS: The International Institute of Medical
             Qigong
             P.O. Box 52144
             Pacific Grove, California 93950 USA
PHONE: (831) 646-9399
FAX: (831) 646-0535

Director and Founder of the International Institute of Medical Qigong—U.S.

- Council Board Member—National Qigong Association (U.S.)
- Executive Chairman—National Board of Medical Qigong Examiners (U.S.)
- Council Board Member—World Academic Society of Medical Qigong, (Beijing, China)
Author of several books and numerous articles

Maria Qinyin
ADDRESS: 10255 Parkwood Dr. #1
Cupertino, California 95014
PHONE: 408-257-7602
FAX: 408-257-7902
EMAIL: *qinyin@earthlink.net*
WEB SITE: *http://home.earthlink.net/~qinyin*
Qigong Master and Founder of Qin-Way to Health and Sublimation

Kenneth S. Cohen, M.A.
ADDRESS: Director
The Qigong Research and Practice Center
P.O. Box 1727
Nederland, Colorado 80466
PHONE/FAX: (303) 258-0971 voice/fax

Author of *The Way of Qigong: The Art and Science of Chinese Energy Healing* (Ballantine, 1997), the Sounds True Qigong audio and video courses (303) 665-3151,

(800) 333-9185, and more than 150 journal articles.

Lecturer sponsored by the American Cancer Society, the Canadian Ministry of Health and numerous universities.

A world leader in the dialogue between Eastern wisdom and Western Science and was one of nine "exceptional healers" tested in experiments at the Menninger Institute.

Sounds True

Audio: Chi Kung Meditations,Taoist Healing Imagery, Healthy Breathing, The Practice of Qigong, Taoism: Essential Teachings, Video:

Qigong: Traditional Chinese Exercises for Healing the Body, Mind, and Spirit. Qigong training, workshops and educational materials.

Barbara Bernic

ADDRESS: Chairman/CEO
American Foundation of Traditional
Chinese Medicine
505 Beach Street
San Francisco, California
PHONE: (415) 776-0502
EMAIL: *aftcm@earthlink.net*

Richard H. Lee

ADDRESS: President
            China Healthways Institute
            115 North El Camino Real
            San Clemente, California 92672
PHONE: (800) 743-5608 / (714) 498-0947
FAX: (714) 498-0947
WEB PAGE: *http://chinahealthways.com*

CHI manufactures and sells various high-technology health products including the Qigong Machine, Kirlian cameras, the "Chi-onizer"

Dr. Zhi Chen Guo

ADDRESS: Hebei Province, China
PHONE: 86-311-802-6979 x 8107
FAX: 86-311-802-3797
WEB PAGE: *http://www.mastersha.com*

Qigong Master and director of Zhe Neng Medicine Clinic.

Dr. Zhi Gang Sha

ADDRESS: Sha's Health Center
            3195 Granville Street, Suite 1
            Vancouver, BC Canada V6H 3K2
PHONE: (888) 339-6815
FAX: (604) 733-0857
WEB PAGE: *http://www.mastersha.com*
BOOKS: *Zhe Neng Medicine, Soul Study, Sha's
            Golden Healing Ball*

Numerous audiotapes and videos are also available from Master Sha.

Effie Poy Yew Chow, Ph.D., R.N., Dipl.Ac. (NACCA), Lic.Ac.

ADDRESS: President,
East West Academy of Healing Arts
450 Sutter Street, Suite 2104
San Francisco, California 94108
PHONE: (415) 788-2227
FAX: (415) 788-2242
EMAIL: *eastwestqi@aol.com*
WEB PAGE: *http://www.eastwestqi.com/*
Qigong Master

To order the book *Qigong: Miracle Healing from China*, audio- or videotapes, call 1-800-824-2433.

Kenneth M. Sancier, Ph.D.

ADDRESS: President
The Qigong Institute
561 Berkeley Avenue
Menlo Park, California 94025
PHONE: (650) 323-1221
FAX: (650) 323-1221
EMAIL: *qigonginstitute@healthy.net*
WEB PAGE: *http://www.qigonginstitute.org*

The Qigong Institute is a nonprofit organization with numerous audiotapes as well as a computer database of over thirteen hundred scientific abstracts on Qigong research.

Andreas Kuehne

ADDRESS: Qigong & Kung Fu Instruction
                     Am Heizkraftwerk 6
                     17235 Neustrelitz
                     East Germany
EMAIL: *thammavong@mvnet.de*

Roger Jahnke, O.M.D.

WEB SITE: *http://www.Healthy.Net/Qigong*
EMAIL: *rjahnke@west.net*

                 Doctor of Oriental Medicine
                 Senior Faculty at the Santa Barbara
                 College of Oriental Medicine

Author of *The Healer Within*, published by HarperCollins. Keynotes, lectures, retreats, training. Information and ordering: 800-824-4325.

Garri Garripoli

WEB SITE: *http://www.WujiProductions.com*
BOOKS: *Qigong: Essence of the Healing Dance* and
                 Tao of the Ride
VIDEOS: The Public Television documentary,
                 Qigong: Ancient Chinese Healing for the
                 21st Century, and *The Wuji Qigong*
                 Instructional home video series
TRIPS: Garri organizes Qigong study trips
                 to China every year.
                 Toll-free order-only line is (800) 723-1927.

Index

About the Author

Garri Garripoli, director/producer of the public television documentary *Qigong: Ancient Chinese Healing for the 21st Century*, has practiced Qigong and Eastern healing arts for over twenty years. He left a full scholarship in premed at the University of Colorado during the mid-1970s to study with a renowned Master of Eastern healing in Hawaii.

His varied work for public television earned him an Emmy Award and reflects his passionate studies in Traditional Chinese Medicine and alternative healing modalities. He has traveled extensively throughout China and Tibet, writing books, television and film scripts, as well as articles for martial arts magazines.

He is also the author of *Tao of the Ride: Motorcycles and the Mechanics of the Soul* (Health Communications, Inc., 1999).

Please visit his Web site:
www.WujiProductions.com

Also from Garri Garripoli –

The Tao of the Ride

"Balance goes beyond the ability to not topple over. I see so many people seeking balance who are caught in the duality trap-viewing life as an either/or predicament-falling over or not falling over. I liken it to my initial bike-riding experience. I learned the essence of the Ride lies in balancing the multitude of factors that you face in life. The duality trap-how many times do we see only two alternatives to a situation? Winning or losing, good or bad, black or white."

—Garri Garripoli

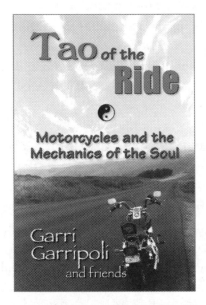

A deft interpretation of the two worlds of motorcycling and Eastern spirituality, and the relationship between them. Garri Garripoli illustrates the *Ride of Life* as it relates to the motorcycle and riding. To that end, the metaphor of motorcycling, which requires balance, acceptance and evenly flowing energy, illustrates the timeless principles of Eastern spirituality, including such Chinese philosophies and concepts as Tao and Qi. Whether you hail from the beat generation or generation X, whether you drive a Fatboy or a minivan, if you enjoy Eastern philosophy and crave a better, more down-to-earth understanding of it, you'll love this book.

Code #6706 Paperback • $9.95

New Chicken Soup for the Soul

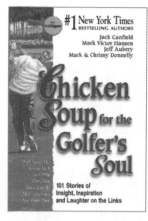

Chicken Soup for the Golfer's Soul

This inspiring collection of stories from professionals, caddies and amateur golfers shares the memorable moments of the game—when, despite all odds, an impossible shot lands in the perfect position; when a simple game of golf becomes a lesson in life. Chapters include: sportsmanship, family, overcoming obstacles, perfecting the game and the nineteenth hole. This is a great read for any golfer, no matter what their handicap.

Code #6587 • $12.95

A 6th Bowl of Chicken Soup for the Soul

This latest batch of wisdom, love and inspiration will warm your hearts and nourish your souls, whether you're "tasting" *Chicken Soup* for the first time, or have dipped your "spoon" many times before.

In the tradition of all the books in the original *Chicken Soup* series, this volume focuses on love; parents and parenting; teaching and learning; death and dying; perspective; overcoming obstacles; and eclectic wisdom. Contributors to *A 6th Bowl of Chicken Soup for the Soul* include: Erma Bombeck, Edgar Guest, Jay Leno, Rachel Naomi Remen, Robert A. Schuller, Dr. James Dobson, Dolly Parton and Cathy Rigby.

Code #6625 • $12.95

Visionary Fiction from HCI